The Simple 6™

A Writing Rubric for Kids

Revised 2nd Edition

by Kay Davidson

Pieces of Learning

© 2009 Pieces of Learning
2nd Revised Edition
CLC0444
ISBN 978-1-934358-21-4
© 2004 1st Edition
Marion IL
Cover Design John Steele

Dedication

To Bill, who encourages me to be me.

Acknowledgments

Special thanks to:

Steve Van Bruaene, my principal, who believed in The Simple 6™
long before a book was even thought of.

My colleagues: Jeanie Butterfield, Joyce Underly, Marilyn Brokaw,
Tressa Decker, Jane Weaver, Bette Diamond, Wally Niemann,
Carleen Dils, Greg Vogel, Greg Diamond, Linda Magnuson,
Caryn Ellison, Karol Leiter, and Liz Warner,
who have put these ideas into practice
and have provided me with data and support.

My undergraduate students from Saint Marys College,
who helped to collect the state data.

Carolyn Coil,
for her professional support and personal guidance
in helping to get this book published.

Kathy Balsamo, my editor, for her expertise, guidance, and
ability to ask simple questions
that yield pages of new ideas.

Table of Contents

The hardest part is getting started **43**

Do you have two hours a week?

By spending an hour a day, two days a week, students quickly master the skills of writing, scoring, and editing. Teaching the strategies one at a time, and adding a new one each week, makes mastery easy. These lesson plans will get you started.

Getting Started. . . The Lessons

It takes practice and variation **126**

What should we ask students to write about? **126**

Sample writing prompts are given as well as tips for collaborating with colleagues to design your own prompts. Students learn to assess and edit pieces of writing in small groups.

Chapter 5 **Expanding Successes for Secondary Students** 142

Same Ideas — Just a Little More Sophisticated 143

Students in grades 6 through 10 are assessed with a rubric that is somewhat more sophisticated but very similar to the one for younger students. Using the elementary rubric for at-risk high school students has many benefits.

An Overview of The Simple 6™

The Simple 6™: A Writing Rubric for Kids simplifies the understanding of how student writing is assessed. For years, classroom teachers have introduced students to the traditional steps of the writing process. Without focusing on the assessment benchmarks and the specific scoring rubrics, however, student achievement consistently falls below expected levels. The general concept of rubric scoring is discussed here as well as an analysis of the rubric used on many state writing assessments.

Most teachers feel overwhelmed by the prospect of improving student writing achievement because they have no direction. The Simple 6™: A Writing Rubric for Kids details specific strategies for writing instruction and improvement. Step-by-step, teachers are introduced to strategies that will not only enhance student understanding but will also increase test scores. Students learn strategies for sticking to the topic, for having logical order, for including interesting words, for using different sentence patterns, for creating descriptive sentences, and for writing for a specific audience. Lesson plans for weekly writing blocks are described in detail. Dialogue takes the teacher through the specific steps, leading students to the mastery level. Suggestions for various teaching strategies are given, and sample writing prompts are included.

At a slightly higher level, The Simple 6™ for Secondary Students is designed for students in grades 6 through 12. An analysis of the scoring rubric illustrates the correlation between The Simple 6™ and the traditional 6-point rubric. The discussion also highlights the use of the elementary rubric for low-achieving secondary students. Simplicity continues to be the instructional focus. The Simple 6™ for Secondary Students is available as a separate book from Pieces of Learning www.piecesoflearning.com.

In both books Language-in-Use is addressed as a separate entity, because on standardized achievement tests it is assessed on a separate rubric. Conventions such as capitalization, punctuation, verb agreement, and spelling are discussed at various grade levels. An illustration shows how state standards parallel the benchmark assessments. You're the Teacher: Editing for Kids shows teachers how to improve student achievement in editing.

The Simple 6™: A Writing Rubric for Kids is a straight-forward, no-nonsense approach to writing instruction and assessment. The program has given my students a sense of understanding and pride because they know what is expected of them. It has given my colleagues a great deal of satisfaction because all their hard work yields positive results. Based on the enthusiasm I've seen and the favorable comments I have received from staff development participants, I am certain that this book will be a valuable resource for teachers who are trying to improve student achievement in the writing process.

Chapter 1

The Writing Process
as We Know It

Is it time to rethink what we've been doing?

What are we missing?

Analytic Rubrics

Holistic Rubrics

Meeting the Challenge

Chapter 1   The Writing Process as We Know It

Is it time to rethink what we've been doing?

When I was in the 6th grade, I was asked to write a story about an animal. I vividly remember being unable to finish this assignment and panicking during the time I was supposed to be writing. Why? Because I didn't know what to write about. I had too many ideas, or not enough ideas. I didn't have a pet, nor did I like animals. Any knowledge about the animals I'd seen in the zoo was limited, so my mind raced through a million possible scenarios which got me no place fast. I had a topic, but I didn't know what to write.

Teachers have been assigning writing topics just like the animal story for a long time. Many have even attempted to teach the writing process. Too often, however, teachers have "done their own thing" when it comes to writing. Some provide their students with daily time for free writing in journals that will never be critiqued or revised. Others believe that every piece of writing should be strictly evaluated and marked in red — to be done over and over and over until perfection has been reached. Some teachers give prompts, while many let students choose their topics. There are teachers everywhere who enthusiastically accept the challenge of teaching their students to write, but many dread it so much that they never get to it.

There are certainly variations of the writing process, but the focus is traditionally on:

- brainstorming and gathering ideas
- organizing your thoughts
- writing the first draft
- letting it sit overnight
- revising, sharing, editing
- writing the final draft
- publishing in some way

Teachers have used these steps for years because they provide a logical, accepted procedure for teaching writing. So why are the majority of students producing pieces of writing that fail to meet the current writing standards? What can be done to improve our students' understanding of the writing process? How can we attempt to improve student achievement in writing and ultimately the assessment results on standardized tests? Recognizing the problem is the first step in solving it.

What are we missing?

In looking at the steps of the writing process, we see a format for teachers and students to follow; but do we really address actual **content?** We seem to have a frame without a picture, a skeleton without a body, a car without an engine . . . and students without real direction. What motivation do students need before they can brainstorm on their own? What is the best way to teach students to organize their thoughts? What makes a story interesting? How can we teach students to appeal to their senses as they write? Why is audience important? There is so much more to writing than just assigning a topic and giving time in class to write.

Realizing that not enough time is being spent on actual content is only one half of the solution. The "bigger half" is our lack of knowledge and understanding of the assessment process itself. It is not easy for most classroom teachers to assign a score to something as subjective as writing. What is the fairest way to do it? Teachers score writing in as many ways as they teach it. The check-plus, the letter-grade, the percentage score, and the pass-fail method are just a few. There has never been a universal scoring method for student writing in the classroom.

Then along came standardized assessment and something called a rubric. The time had come for teachers to make some decisions (and maybe even changes!) They suddenly needed to ask themselves:

* Should I change the way I have
  been grading my students' writing
  all these years?

* Should I ease up with the red pen?

* Should I give students more choice in their
  writing?

* And finally, should I let the standardized
  assessment rubric guide my instruction?

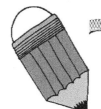

**And by the way . . .
what is a rubric?**

In its simplest form,
a rubric is really
nothing more
than a checklist.
It is used
to **guide** students
toward the teacher's
expectations
and/or
to **evaluate**
the degree of excellence
of the project.

When I first heard the term rubric, a science notebook immediately came to mind. How many times have you assigned a notebook at the end of a unit of study and told students in advance what you expected to be in it? The list of expectations that was given to your students was a rubric. If you took it one step further and told them the number of points they would receive for various degrees of performance on the completed project, you also provided them with a rubric. Not only were students able to use the rubric as a guide during the completion of the project, but they were made fully aware of how their work would be assessed.

The function of a rubric is either developmental or summative. Developmental rubrics are used to assess ongoing student progress. They are designed to highlight student strengths and weaknesses, and are, therefore, valuable tools for identifying areas that need attention. Over time, teachers can track the overall progress of a particular student while simultaneously focusing on skill areas.

Summative rubrics, on the other hand, are used to assess final products. They guide teachers (and students) through a list of performance criteria that yield a final score. Students know in advance what is expected, and teachers find scoring more objective because expectations are specific. Rubrics, however, have different formats. They can be structured analytically or holistically.

Analytic Rubrics

In an analytic rubric, the evaluation of each performance criterion can stand alone. In this type of rubric, the scores may be averaged or used individually to focus on specific skill exemplars or deficiencies. Complex analytic rubrics are the most complete, accurate indicators of student achievement; however, time consumption and difficulty level keep teachers from developing and using them on a regular basis. All analytic rubrics are not complex, however.

Simple Analytic Rubrics

FRIENDLY LETTER RUBRIC			
	Not mastered (0)	**Mastered (1)**	**Points**
Heading			
Greeting			
Body			
Closing			
Signature			
		Total Points	

This simple analytic rubric can be quick and effective. Total points can easily be transferred to a percentage or letter grade.

Simple analytic rubrics are also valuable assessment tools for evaluating writing exercises that would not necessarily receive a letter grade. Consider this rubric which evaluates a reading response entry in a journal.

READING RESPONSE RUBRIC			
	Unsatisfactory (0)	**Satisfactory (1)**	**Points**
Title/Author/Genre			
Short Summary			
Reflection/Analysis			
		Total Points	

Complex Analytic Rubrics

Complex analytic rubrics evaluate the general degree of various skills. They indicate the overall success of a student product or can be analyzed by specific criterion. They are highly effective in evaluating projects, products, and presentations with precise accuracy.

SCIENCE NOTEBOOK RUBRIC					
	Score 1 **Minimal**	**Score 2** **Adequate**	**Score 3** **Commendable**	**Score 4** **Outstanding**	**Total Points**
Content	Missing some content	Most required content in included	All required content is included	All required content is included plus additional related material	
Scientific Accuracy	Inaccurate scientific facts or reasoning	Accurate but minimal scientific facts or reasoning	Accurate, detailed scientific facts and reasoning	Accurate, detailed, and illustrated scientific facts and reasoning	
Organization	Format does not follow Table of Contents.	Format mostly follows Table of Contents	Format follows Table of Contents	Format follows Table of Contents	
Neatness	Neatness is lacking.	Many erasures; drawings and diagrams not neat and/or mastered	Few erased errors; drawings and diagrams are colored and measured	No noticeable errors; drawings and diagrams are colored and measured	
Timeliness	Turned in more than one day late	Turned in one day late	Turned in on time	Turned in on time	
				Total Score	

Holistic Rubrics

Holistic rubrics yield one score based on overall performance. In holistic scoring, a list of criteria is cross-referenced with degrees of proficiency. One score is assigned based on the piece's best fit on a rubric chart.

ORAL PRESENTATION RUBRIC			
	Score 1 **Minimal**	**Score 2** **Adequate**	**Score 3** **Commendation**
Organization	Has little order and no interaction with the audience.	Has understandable order but lacks inviting beginning and strong conclusion.	Has logical order with an inviting beginning and a strong conclusion that includes questions from the audience.
Planning	Shows lack of planning.	Shows an attempt at planning.	Shows thorough planning and preparation.
Presentation	Inaudibly reads presentation without making eye contact with the audience.	Speaks clearly, periodically makes eye contact, and attempts to engage the audience.	Speaks in a loud, clear voice, makes eye contact and clearly engages the audience.
Content	Gives incorrect or unclear information that is unsupported by examples.	Gives basic information with minimal examples.	Gives clear information and appropriate examples.
			Score

Complex holistic rubrics are cumbersome and hard to understand. It takes training, practice, and a complete understanding of all rubric elements to use them effectively. Teachers who use complex holistic rubrics must be constantly cross-referencing between criterion and proficiency level to find where the piece precisely fits. Then one score is assigned.

Complex holistic rubrics can also be vague. The terminology used as performance indicators makes it difficult to determine when the piece has moved from one scoring level to the next. Proficiency indicators like _very clear, clear,_ and _somewhat clear_ are too subjective and discourage classroom teachers from using them. Unfortunately, many of the rubrics used to score statewide standardized writing assessments follow this format. Below is an example of a typical rubric used to evaluate student writing.

Standardized Assessment Rubric for Writing Applications						
Score	**1**	**2**	**3**	**4**	**5**	**6**
Content	Has little or no focus on topic. Has few relevant ideas.	Has minimal focus on topic. Has few relevant ideas.	Stays somewhat focused on topic. Has some relevant ideas.	Stays mostly focused on topic. Has many relevant ideas.	Stays focused on topic. Has many relevant ideas.	Stays completely focused on topic. Has thorough and complete ideas.
Organization	Does not organize ideas logically.	Does not organize ideas logically.	Attempts to organize ideas logically.	Organizes ideas logically.	Organizes ideas logically.	Organizes ideas logically.
Style	Shows less than minimal word usage and writing technique.	Shows less than minimal word usage and writing technique.	Shows minimal word usage and writing technique.	Shows adequate word usage and writing technique.	Shows more than adequate word usage and writing technique.	Shows exceptional word usage and writing technique.
Voice	Uses inappropriate language and tone.	Uses inappropriate language and tone.	Attempts to use appropriate language and tone.	Attempts to use appropriate language and tone.	Uses appropriate language and tone.	Uses appropriate language and tone
					Score	

Meeting the Challenge

In general, some type of complex holistic rubric is the assessment tool being used to evaluate student progress on standardized assessments. Even though they frequently come with explanations and anchor papers to validate the scoring, they are not easy to understand; and because students sometimes receive only one numeric score on their assessment, it is difficult to learn from the experience.

Whether classroom teachers agree with the process and understand it is beside the point. Students have a right to know it; and teachers have a responsibility to learn it, to use it regularly in class, and to make students aware of its components. Do you know and understand the rubric that is being used to evaluate your students on standardized writing assessments? More importantly, have you taken the time to share this method of assessment with your students?

Some states have encouraged classroom teachers to become familiar with the writing assessment process and have provided booklets to familiarize teachers and parents with the scoring procedure. In general, though, teachers are not familiar enough with the process to carry it into the classroom effectively, and the rubrics are often confusing. Nevertheless, this information is available to teachers and parents from the state departments of education by writing to them or visiting their web sites.

The Simple 6™: A Writing Rubric for Kids is based on information derived from the study and analysis of the complex holistic writing rubrics used for standardized assessment. By taking a close look at the exemplars in the highest scoring papers (and not focusing on the holistic rubric), the qualities that make an outstanding piece begin to surface.

Stick to the Topic
Logical Order
Interesting Words
Different Sentence
    Patterns
Descriptive Sentences
Audience

Chapter 2

Simplifying Rubric Scoring
Using The Simple 6™

If you look closely, is it really all that complicated?

Pretest: Writing Assessment

Identifying the Qualities of Outstanding Writing

Scoring Descriptions

The Simple 6™ as a Complex Holistic Rubric

The Simple 6™ as a Simple Analytic Rubric

Quick Reference Chart for Elementary

Taking a Look at Each Component of the Rubric

My Writing Record

© 2009 Pieces of Learning
The Simple 6™ Revised Edition

Chapter 2 Simplifying Rubric Scoring Using The Simple 6™

If you look closely, is it really all that complicated?

The most intimidating factor in the scoring rubrics used across the United States is the jargon that identifies the rubric headings. Typically, the components being assessed are **content**, **organization**, **style**, **voice**, and **conventions**. Now, let's be realistic and think about these words. Are their meanings easy for students to understand? Consider the types of students who will be taking the standardized assessment:

- **your typical second grader,** who is probably seven years old, learning to write paragraphs for the first time, preparing for the assessment which could be given as early as the fall of third grade

- **your below average fifth grader,** who has difficulty not only in decoding those words, but also in being able to understand what they mean

- **your above average middle school student,** who writes well, but has no knowledge or understanding of the words or the rubric in general

- **your at-risk high school student,** who has difficulty reading, spelling, and organizing thoughts. In addition you may be dealing with a negative attitude and the stress (or not) about whether the student will graduate because of the inability to pass this assessment

- **your student with special needs,** and an individualized education plan, who also has to show proficiency in writing on state assessments

- **your student who is learning English** as a new language

The key to understanding anything is to break instructional concepts into components that students can apply to their own learning. The rubric is no exception. Imagine asking your students to write the definitions for each of those terms. From most students' point of view, the concepts are unknown or too vague to describe. By simplifying the ideas, however, students will understand them. By practicing on a regular basis, they will improve. By learning to assess their own writing, they will achieve success. Can they do it under the present conditions? Give this pretest to see how much your students really understand about writing expectations.

Name _____   Date _____

Pretest: Writing Assessment

Directions: Your writing this year will be evaluated in the following areas.
Tell what each word means, and give an example of how you might show
your proficiency in that area.

content: _____

example: _____

_____

organization: _____

example:

_____

_____

style: _____

example:

_____

_____

voice: _____

example:

_____

_____

conventions:_____
example:

_____

_____

Identifying the Qualities of Outstanding Writing

Let's consider **simplifying** the entire process. This can be done by closely examining the categories of ideas and content, organization, and style/voice. What is really being assessed in each of these areas?

Ideas and Content

A student who has outstanding ideas and content has fully **focused on the topic** and hasn't rambled or repeated himself. He has explored the topic fully by answering the questions in the prompt and has provided specific information in his supporting details.

Organization

Organization is clearly evident. There is a clear sequence of beginning, middle, and end. The introduction and conclusion are strong, and the **logical order** totally supports the topic.

Style

The writer exhibits style by using **exceptional vocabulary** that creates **vivid descriptions** *with rich details.* **Varied sentence patterns** make the writing sound natural; its fluency makes it easy to understand. The writer displays a strong sense of audience by showing his emotions or personality. His unique perspective makes this piece of writing exemplary in every way.

By focusing on specific elements in each broad category, it is easy to identify the exact skills that students must master to show proficiency in writing. These 6 specific elements make up <u>The Simple 6 ™: A Writing Rubric for Kids.</u> The elements are highlighted in the scoring descriptions on the next page.

Scoring Descriptions

6 A Score 6 paper is an outstanding performance and therefore is rare.

- sticks to the topic
- has logical order (with developed introduction and strong conclusion)
- uses interesting vocabulary
- uses different sentence patterns
- has descriptive sentences
- writes for a specific audience

5 The difference between a Score 6 and a Score 5 paper is often the degree of in-depth development and the use of descriptive, supporting details.

- sticks to the topic
- has logical order (and strong conclusion)
- uses interesting vocabulary
- uses different sentence patterns
- writes for a specific audience

4 A Score 4 paper represents a "passing" performance. One factor that differentiates between a Score 4 and a higher score is the lack of ideas and content. A Score 4 frequently lacks the organizational qualities of a Score 5 or Score 6. One example might include:

- sticks to the topic
- has logical order
- uses interesting vocabulary
- uses different sentence patterns

3 A Score 3 paper is associated with the word minimal. It has a definite, list-like quality with little or no development of ideas. One example might include:

- sticks to the topic
- has logical order
- uses interesting vocabulary

2 A Score 2 attempts to communicate some ideas. The content, however, is never really developed.

- attempts to stick to the topic
- attempts to provide descriptive sentences

1 A Score 1 paper attempts to address the prompt. Problems with sentence construction and development of ideas seriously compromise meaning.

- attempts to stick to the topic

If The Simple 6™ were a complex holistic rubric it might look like this:

THE SIMPLE 6™: A WRITING RUBRIC FOR KIDS					
	1 Poor	**3 Minimal**	**5 Competent**	**6 Exemplary**	**Total**
Topic	Attempts sticking to the topic	Sticks to the topic	Sticks to the topic	Sticks to the topic	
Logical Order	Lacks order	Has order	Has order with a developed beginning, middle, and end	Has order with a developed beginning, middle, and end	
Interesting Words	Lacks interesting words	Attempts interesting words	Has several challenging words	Has an abundance of challenging words	
Sentence Patterns	Lacks varied sentence patterns	Has sentences with list-like quality	Varies sentence patterns	Varies sentence patterns to enhance fluency	
Descriptive Sentences	Lacks descriptive sentences	Attempts descriptive sentences	Uses descriptions and examples	Has rich descriptions that appeal to the senses	
Audience	Lacks audience connection	Lacks audience connection	Attempts to connect with audience	Writes for a specific audience or with unique style	
				Total	

© Kay Davidson

This rubric follows the format of traditional scoring. It can and should be attached to the student writing that is being assessed. Complex holistic rubrics are difficult, however, for students and teachers to use effectively. They require the scorer to look at all components at once to find the line that best fits the piece, and after scoring it is difficult to identify specific weaknesses that could impact future instruction.

However, The Simple 6™ is not designed to be used as a complex holistic rubric. It is a simple analytic rubric that can initially be presented to students as questions.

Name _____   Date _____

A Writing Rubric for Kids

Stick to the topic.

Check for logical order.

Include interesting words.

Use different sentence patterns.

Write descriptive sentences.

Write for an audience.

Ask these questions:

yes = 1 point   no= 0 points

_____   Did you **stick to the topic**, or did you run away with some other idea?

_____   Have you presented your thoughts in a **logical order** that included an inviting beginning and a strong conclusion?

_____   Have you overused generic vocabulary, or have you gone back to look for opportunities to use **interesting words**?

_____   Did you use **different sentence patterns**, or does your story sound like a list?

_____   Does each paragraph have a topic sentence and supporting detail **sentences that are descriptive**?

_____   Did you write for an **audience**? (original, lively, or another unique perspective appropriate for the prompt)

_____   **TOTAL POINTS** (How many did you answer yes?)

© 2009 Pieces of Learning
The Simple 6™ Revised Edition

Many state writing assessments score their prompts using a 6-point scale, so why not identify 6 mastery skills? Students now have a direct correlation between what is being asked of them, and how, specifically, they can improve their writing. Students learn the 6 components of exemplary writing as simple phrases. They are easy to remember, so students automatically review this mental checklist as they write, prepare for revision, edit, and complete their piece.

Are these the only 6 items that the assessment team is looking for? Not necessarily. Will addressing each of these items guarantee a score of 6? Probably not, because a Score 6 is exceedingly exemplary in every way and is seldom given. (It is not impossible, however, and it should still be your goal!) Will mastery of these 6 concepts guarantee improvement? Yes. Will it guide teachers in a definite direction? Yes. Will it provide students with the necessary skills and understanding to pass a standardized writing assessment? Yes. Why? Because students now know exactly what the total package looks like in an outstanding piece of writing.

If you **STICK TO THE TOPIC** in your writing, the reader will focus on the main idea.

If you have structured your writing with **LOGICAL ORDER**, the reader will be able to follow and understand your message.

If you include **INTERESTING WORDS** (challenging vocabulary), you will sound as intelligent as you really are.

If you have chosen **DIFFERENT SENTENCE PATTERNS**, your writing will not sound like a list.

If you have written **DESCRIPTIVE SENTENCES**, the reader will be able to visualize what you are trying to say.

If you have connected with the **AUDIENCE**, then what you have written has made an impact.

The bottom line is this: Not many teachers are going to reach mastery in traditional, holistic rubric scoring. So let's take a closer look at what assessment professionals are really looking for in an exemplary piece of writing — in plain English.

The Simple 6™

Quick Reference Chart for Elementary

Stick to the Topic

- Stick to the topic, and don't run away with other ideas.
- Follow the prompt instructions.

Logical Order

- BME (Beginning, Middle, End)
- Focus on the strong conclusion.
- Use the prompt to guide structure.

Interesting Words

- Include 3 challenging vocabulary attempts. (minimum)
- Eliminate generic words like *went* and *said*.
- Replace words used many times.
- Use words specific to this topic.

Different Sentence Patterns

- Include questions, exclamations, and items in a series.
- Focus on compound/complex sentences.
- Create fluency as a result.

Descriptive Sentences

- Use precise verbs.
- Include proper nouns.
- Insert adjectives
- Appeal to the reader's senses.

Audience

- Write in a tone that is appropriate for the prompt.
- Let your personality shine! (exclamations, thoughts, questions, humor, satire)

The Simple 6™ A Writing Rubric for Kids

Taking a Look at Each Component of the Rubric

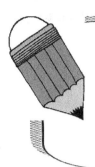

Stick to the Topic

- Stick to the topic, and don't ramble and repeat.
- Follow the prompt instructions.

Writing Prompt

Topic: Hungry Harley

Your cat has run out of cat food.
What will you do?

Be sure to include:
- What kind of food he likes
- Where you will get it
- How you will get there
- Ideas that stick with this topic

Does your writing look like this?

> My cat needed some food. His name is Harley. He is very lively, and he always gets into trouble. He only likes Purrrrr-Fecto Cat Food so I bought 6 cans. I will keep it on the shelf in the basement. Our basement is very messy!

Or this?

> My cat Harley needed some food. He's very picky about what he eats, so I had to wait until my mom got home from work so she could drive me to Kitty Mart. They sell Purrrr-Fecto Cat Food, and that is his favorite. Luckily, they had plenty of it when I got there. I bought 6 cans and rushed home. I knew Harley would be waiting at the door.

Ideas for <u>Stick to the Topic</u>

This topic lends itself to nouns: people, places, and things. Always choose a topic with which students have knowledge or experience. Narrative writing is the easiest place to start. Write your own ideas in the spaces provided.

<u>Family Topics:</u>
　　Examples: Being in My Family is _____
　　　　　　　The Best Brother (or Sister) OR
　　　　　　　I Wish I Had a Brother or Sister

<u>School Topics:</u>
　　Examples: I (Don't) Like School
　　　　　　　The Best School

<u>Age-related Topics:</u>
　　Examples: I Need an Allowance
　　　　　　　I'm Old Enough to _____

<u>Literature-based Topics:</u>
　　Examples: The Bravest Moment
　　　　　　　The Day I Found a _____
　　　　　　　Making Choices
　　　　　　　I Remember when _____

<u>Science Topics:</u>
　　Examples: Amphibians
　　　　　　　The Process of Photosynthesis
　　　　　　　How Electricity was Discovered

<u>Social Studies/Current Event Topics:</u>
　　Examples: Being a Good citizen
　　　　　　　If I were President
　　　　　　　The Boston Tea Party

© 2009 Pieces of Learning
The Simple 6™ Revised Edition

Logical Order

- BME (Beginning, Middle, End)
- Focus on the strong conclusion.
- Use the prompt to guide structure.

Writing Prompt

Topic: Get up, Sleepy Head!

Most people have a regular routine that they follow every morning.
What did you do this morning before you came to school?

Be sure to include:
- How you felt
- What you did (in order!)
- How you got to school
- A beginning, a middle, and an ending

Does your writing look like this?

I didn't want to come to school today. I was tired, but my mom made me come. I didn't have my homework done. It was still sitting on the kitchen table. I knew I would get in trouble. My mom was waiting in the car so I grabbed some juice. I got dressed too.

Or this?

The alarm went off at 7:30. I didn't want to come to school today, but my mom made me. I was so tired from doing homework. I got up, brushed my teeth, took a shower, and got dressed. When I went downstairs, I saw my homework sitting on the kitchen table, so I hurried and packed it up. Mom was already waiting in the driveway, so I grabbed some juice and hopped into the car!

Ideas for <u>Logical Order</u> Topics

Focus on expository writing. These paragraphs or stories tell what happened, how to do or make something, or how to get somewhere. Retelling stories is also an effective way to introduce or practice putting events in logical order.

Book Reviews or Summaries

What happened when . . .

How do you make . . . (an interesting recipe or a craft project)

How would you get from — to —

Tell me about the new movie . . .

Other Ideas for Logical Order:

_____

_____

_____

_____

_____

_____

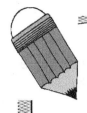

Interesting Words (Challenging Vocabulary)

- Include 3 challenging vocabulary attempts.
- Eliminate generic words like <u>went</u> and <u>said</u>.
- Replace words used many times.
- Use words specific to this topic.

Writing Prompt

Topic: What Did You See Today?

On my way to school this morning
I noticed . . .

Be sure to include:
- Where you were
- What your saw
- Interesting words

Does your writing look like this?

This morning I saw some birds. They were in the yard. I think they were looking for worms because they kept trying to eat the grass. As I walked toward them they flew away.

Or this?

It was a gorgeous morning so I decided to take a leisurely walk to school. On my way I noticed three busy robins. They suddenly appeared in my neighbor's yard under their ancient oak tree. I think they were searching for worms, because they kept pecking frantically at the wet grass. As I crept toward them they soared away, leaving their breakfast behind.

Ideas for <u>Interesting Words</u> Topics

Any and every kind of writing can contain interesting (challenging) words. When writing about topics that have specific vocabulary, you may want to start with a word bank.

Sports/Gymnastics/Dance/Games
Example: The Big Game

Holidays
Example: The Christmas I'll Always Remember

Science Topics
Example: The Life of a Snake

History Topics
Example: Martin Luther King's Dream

Current Events
Example: Why Everyone Should Vote

Theme Parks/Vacation Spots
Example: My Day at _____

Other Ideas for Interesting Words:

_____

_____

_____

_____

_____

_____

Different Sentence Patterns

- Include questions, exclamations, and items in a series.
- Focus on compound/complex sentences.
- Use direct quotations if appropriate.
- Create fluency as a result.

Writing Prompt

Topic: My Family

Families come in different shapes and sizes, and no two are ever exactly alike. Write a story about your family that includes the members of your family, where you live, and what you like to do together.

Does your writing look like this?

My family is nice. I have a big house and we all live there. I have one brother and two sisters. I have a Mom and Dad too. I have the best family in the world.

Or this?

Have you ever met my family? There are six of us, and we all live together in an old, gigantic, two-story farmhouse. My brother's name is Joe, my two older sisters are Susan and Julie, and I am Taylor. We all love animals, so Mom and Dad got a house in the country. Being in this family is the greatest!

Ideas for <u>Different Sentence Patterns</u> Topics

The topic doesn't matter. This is a good time, however, to take out an old piece of writing. Look closely at the sentence patterns. Can you revise them using the new strategies?

<u>Example 1</u>

I like to go shopping with my mom. We go every Saturday. We go to the mall and then we go out for lunch. We always buy stuff that is on sale. We always have a good time and then we do it again the next week.

<u>Example 2</u>

Dinosaurs are interesting. Dinosaurs lived millions of years ago. Dinosaurs eat plants but some dinosaurs eat other dinosaurs. Some dinosaurs were very huge, and some dinosaurs were very tiny. Dinosaurs also are not alive today.

<u>Example 3</u>

School is fun. I like it because my friends are there. I like learning about new things in all our subjects. I like my teacher. She is nice. She makes school fun. I like the food in the cafeteria and the principal. I like school better than anything else in the world.

Other Ideas for Different Sentence Patterns:

_____

_____

_____

_____

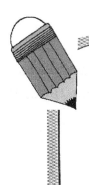

Descriptive Sentences

- Use precise verbs.
- Include proper nouns.
- Insert adjectives.
- Appeal to the reader's senses.

Writing Prompt

Topic: The Championship Game

Last night your team won the champion ship game. Write a story about this thrilling event that includes the kind of game, where it was played, and all the exciting details.

Does your writing look like this?

> Last night our basketball team played in the championship game. A lot of people came. They yelled and cheered for the team. We finally won. Then we went home.

Or this?

> Last night our basketball team, the Twin Branch Tigers, played the Beiger Bulldogs in the championship game. Our gym was so packed! It was exciting, but it made me nervous too. The score was close most of the game, and the crowd went wild when we tied with ten seconds left.
>
> Finally, I hit an open shot — nothing but the net — to win the game! It was the most exciting night of my life, but I was so exhausted I went straight home and went to bed.

Ideas for <u>Descriptive Sentences</u> Topics

There is no need for you to write a whole paragraph to focus on descriptive sentences. Just take a look at one sentence at a time. Give students the easy one. Help them revise to the quality of the second one.

One day I found a dollar bill.

One lucky day I discovered an old, wrinkled, dollar bill on the sidewalk.

I saw a bird this morning.

I noticed the most beautiful robin first thing this morning.

My brother likes brownies.

My brother Joe absolutely adores Mrs. Baker's Chocolate Chip Brownies.

The teacher lost her pencil.

Yesterday Mrs. Weaver misplaced her new, silver pencil with the white eraser.

That clown looks funny.

That tall clown with the frizzy hair looks so hilarious.

That toy is broken.

That old toy truck was destroyed when my brother carelessly stepped on it.

I have new shoes.

I just purchased new, neon blue and silver Adidas™ that are as fast as lightning!

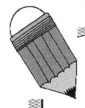

Audience

- Write in a tone that is appropriate for the prompt.
- Let your personality shine! (exclamations, thoughts, questions, humor, satire)

Topic: The Hot Day

What would you do on a hot day?
Who would you do it with?
Where would you go?
How did you feel?

Does your writing look like this?

One hot day my family decided to go to the lake. We all got into the car with our stuff. We took towels, goggles, a beach ball, toys for my baby brother, and a chair for my dad. It was crowded in the car, but we didn't care. After fifteen minutes we pulled into the parking lot, and I raced my sister to the water.

Or this?

Did you know that the temperature was almost one hundred scorching degrees on Saturday? It was so hot that we could hardly stand it, so we talked our parents into taking us to the lake. Trying to get all our stuff into the car wasn't the easiest thing to do, but we managed it. We took towels, goggles, a beach ball, toys for my baby brother, and a lawnchair for my dad. (He HATES the sand!) It was crowded in the car, but we hung our heads out the window and tried not to elbow one another. The last thing we wanted was to have to go back home. After fifteen minutes we pulled into the parking lot, and I raced my sister to the water. "Last one in is a rotten egg!" I yelled, as I skipped over the hot sand.

Idea List for <u>Audience</u> Topics

Topics should include ideas that easily lend themselves to emotion or attitude. Narrative and persuasive writing topics easily motivate students.

Enthusiasm
Example: Something I Really Want to Do

Anger
Example: The Day I Lost My Temper

Sadness
Example: The Saddest Day of My Life

Authority
Example: Dear Mom and Dad,
                I Just Don't Agree . . .

Fear
Example: I was Sooooo Scared!

Embarrassment
Example: My Most Embarrassing Moment

Persuasion
Example: Less Homework

Humor
Example: Now That Was a Laugh!

Other Ideas for Connecting to the Audience:

_____

_____

_____

_____

_____

_____

My Writing Record

Date	

Chapter 3

A Nine-Week Implementation Plan

Getting Started

Weeks 1 - 9 Narratives

Follow-up Lessons for Each Week

Standardized Lesson Plans

Prompt Attack & Mini Rubric Templates

Scoring Analysis and Anchor Papers

Chapter 3   A Nine-Week Implementation Plan

The hardest part is getting started.

It's easy to get started tomorrow. Just take it one step at a time. Major growth can be seen in most students' writing in nine weeks. That's plenty of time for instruction, guided practice, discussion, and sharing. As students improve their writing skills, it is important for them (and you) to be able to document their progress. A simple manilla folder with "My Writing Record" (p.41) attached to the front works well.

If students have a writing folder or binder that they regularly use to keep track of works in progress (like a Writer's Workshop-type folder), keep that separate. This folder is for published work only that follows the progression of *The Simple 6*™ plan. It will be easier to track improvement if you only focus on the pieces that are written each Thursday and Friday. Depending on the age of the students, you can fill in the first topics before you duplicate the progress sheet. Older students can fill them in as they go. Rubber cement or use spray adhesive on the progress sheet and attach it onto a regular file folder. Write student names on the tabs. This can be accomplished in less than 10 minutes.

This chapter is divided into weekly lessons for an entire nine-week grading period. You will need an hour each Thursday and Friday to accomplish the tasks. In-depth narratives explain exactly what to do and are followed by standards-based, formal lesson plans. Why Thursday-Friday? Writing at the end of the week gives students an opportunity to build a content knowledge base throughout the week. What students are reading, learning in the content areas, and experiencing in their world create writing topics that students know about and care about.

What about grammar? Language mechanics skills are determined by the standards, the needs of the students, and their connection to the week's writing focus. I recommend teaching grammar mini-lessons throughout the week, with the focus on content during the Thursday-Friday lessons. Once students have learned The Simple 6™, however, editing and revision skills are combined.If you are enthusiastic about teaching writing skills, you're ready to begin!

Week 1: Stick to the Topic   Day 1/Thursday

Focus only on sticking to the topic. Start with a single-word, concrete topic such as *dogs, pets, friends, family,* or *school.* Any topic in which students have background knowledge will work. Bring students together on the floor and show and/or read several different fiction or nonfiction books about the same topic.

PETS – Nonfiction

Animals at Home by Sonia Black   I Love Guinea Pigs by Dick King-Smith
Pets by Angela Royston

PETS – Fiction

The Tarantula in My Purse by Jean C. George   Arthur's New Puppy by Marc Brown
Can I Keep Him? By Steven Kellogg   Annie's Pet by Barbara Brenner

Discuss their organization. Using a web, brainstorm the contents on the board. Compare the books. Were they alike? *No.* What did they all have in common? *They were all about the same topic.* Make sure all students understand what sticking to the topic means. Ask them to think of question words that might be included on a web to help gather ideas about the topic.

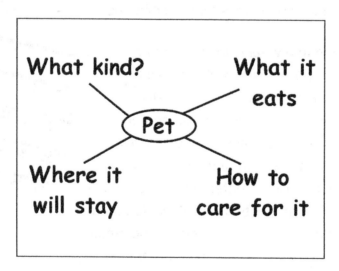

Take this one step further by discussing the following prompt with students:

> **Your parents have told you that you may get a pet. Think about the kind of pet you would like. What would it eat? Where will it stay? How will you care for it?**

It is now time for students to plan their writing. Consider the choices on the following page.

Traditional Brainstorming or Prompt Attack?

Option #1:   Traditional Brainstorming

Give each student a sheet of colored, unlined copy paper. This will be called brainstorming paper from now on. Students will have five minutes (time it!) to web their ideas. All pencils *must keep moving* the entire five minutes. Remember: During brainstorming, all ideas are good ideas!

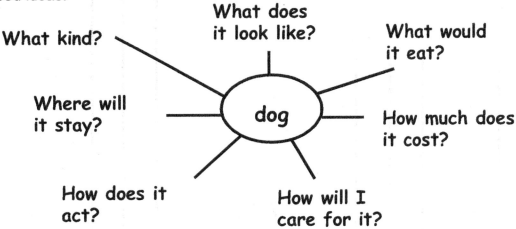

This brainstorming will make an interesting story, but it is not focused on the task being presented in the prompt.

Option #2: Prompt Attack

Review the prompt, focusing on the questions being asked. Using the template on the next page, show students how to web with the actual prompt questions. Students will answer each question in a complete sentence, followed by key words that will remind them of the details they want to include.

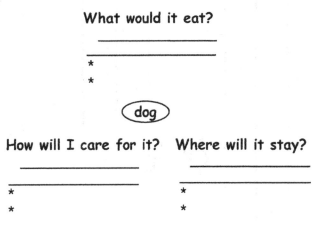

Give students about 10 minutes to write a rough draft on (yellow) lined paper, writing on every other line to make room for future revision. Put students into groups of three to share their stories. If the student sticks to the topic, move to the next. If not, work together to make corrections.

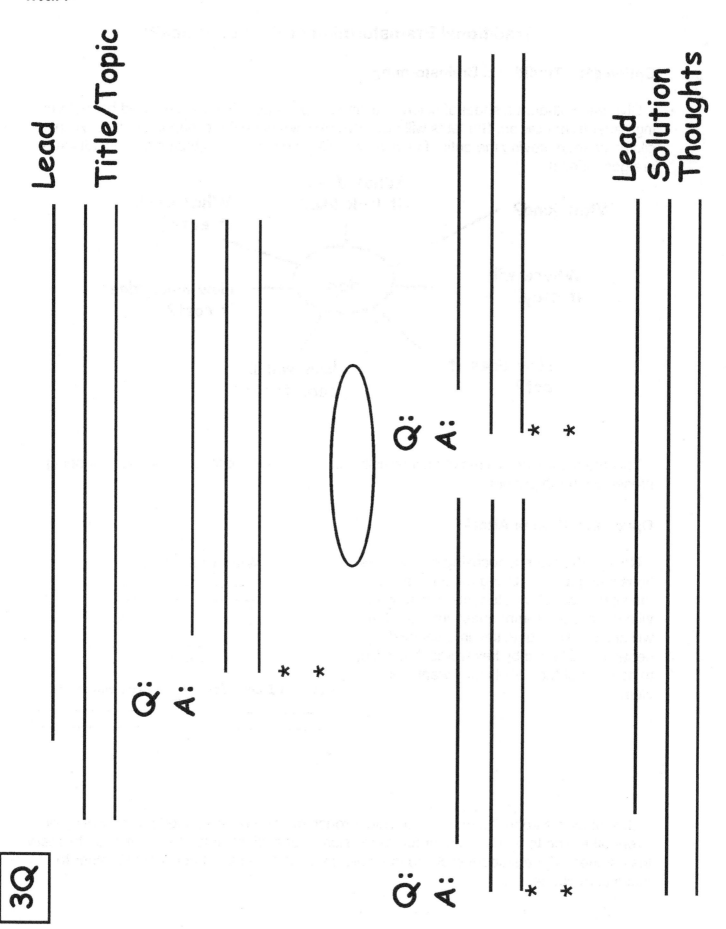

3Q

SAMPLE ROUGH DRAFTS

PLANNING WITH TRADITIONAL BRAINSTORMING

One time I saw a dog in the pet store at the mall. It was barking like crazy! Like it was so exsited to see me. I asked me mom if I could go in and look at it. But she said no because we were in a hury. We had to get some stuf for my scince projekt. We were going to the nacheral wonder store.

PLANNING WITH PROMPT ATTACK

I asked my parents a million times if I could have a pet, and they finally said yes! I didn't have to think about the kind of pet I wanted. I knew right away that it would be a dog. I always wanted a Havernese. It is a very small dog so it will not eat much. It will have to stay in a cage or a box at night. I will have to feed it and play with it. It will be so much fun. I think I will name my new dog Mia.

Week 1: Stick to the Topic   Day 2/Friday

Using the Quick Reference Chart on page 28 review the concept of sticking to the topic. Then share a few stories that you have written.

The Surprise Package

One summer afternoon I was playing tag in the front yard with some friends. I happened to look up and see the mailman coming toward the house. He was carrying an incredibly huge package. I began to wonder if it might be mine, because my birthday is coming up. Actually it's a week away, and I'm going to have a birthday party. I'll probably invite all the friends who are at my house now playing tag. We will have a great time.

In the second example, show a piece that sticks to the topic but has very low-level writing. Then talk about ways in which it might become more interesting, but do not focus on interest at this time.

The Surprise Package

One Saturday morning I was watching tv. I heard the door bell ring. It was the mailman. He brought a big package. I looked on the box to see who it was for. It was for me, so I opened it.

Use an outstanding piece for the third example. Always model exemplary work for your students, and talk them through the writing process as much as you can.

The Surprise Package

The day after my birthday I was a little disappointed. My dad works in sales, and he travels a lot. When he's out of town on my birthday he ALWAYS sends me something special, and it ALWAYS arrives the day before. I suppose it wouldn't be very polite to call him, but I can't help but wonder if he forgot about me.

I reluctantly went to the television and turned on my favorite cartoon show so I could take my mind off the situation. Suddenly, I recognized a familiar car pulling into the driveway. I rushed out side, leaving the front door wide open.

"How's my birthday girl?" yelled Dad. "I'll bet you thought I forgot about you, but I didn't. My plane was delayed because of heavy fog, so I didn't make it home last night."

"Oh, thanks, Dad," I replied. "I knew you'd never forget about me."

Distribute yesterday's papers. Give students time to read their own work to determine if it sounds right. Give them time to make changes. Ask for volunteers to read their stories. At the end of each ask, *"Did he stick to the topic?"* If not, work together to make adjustments and corrections.

Once students have had all their questions answered, give them writing paper for their final drafts. Make sure they understand that the title will be the same as the topic. Why? Because if you stuck to the topic, that's what the story is about! Examples:

I don't know what kind of dog I have. She is just a plain dog, but I don't care. She is frisky and playful, and I love her. She waits for me to come home from school every day.

The next door neighbors have a dog. It is so annoying because it barks constantly. I've never really looked at it much, I just mostly hear it. Sometimes I just want to scream or sleep with my pillow over my head. I wish the neighbors would just take that dog inside!

Week 1: Stick to the Topic   Follow-Up Activities

* Read other stories about similar topics. Brainstorm together. Write a paragraph together on the board that models best practices in sticking to the topic.

* In flexible groups work together with students who need additional practice recognizing sentences that do not stick to the topic. Practice eliminating the sentences that do not belong with teacher-provided paragraphs or actual unidentified student writing from previous years' classes.

* As a writing center activity, with a partner or alone, give students paragraphs that contain sentences that do not stick to the topic. Have students use highlighters to find the sentences that don't belong.

* Focus on the importance of the topic being in the topic sentence. This should be followed by two or three supporting detail sentences. Talk briefly about ending sentences. Choose five students to be the paragraph. The teacher will give the topic. Student 1 is the topic sentence, student 2 is the first supporting detail sentence, and so on. This can be done as a demonstration or in small groups that work simultaneously and then verbally share their paragraphs.

* Practice identifying questions in the prompt that will make up the three body paragraphs.

Your ideas:

_____

_____

_____

_____

_____

_____

_____

_____

_____

_____

Lesson Plan: Stick to the Topic Day 1

Title: **Stick to the Topic**   **Minutes: 60 minutes**
Source: *The Simple 6™: A Writing Rubric for Kids*

Behavioral Objectives: **Students will:**
- create a web about a familiar topic.
- use their web to write a paragraph.

Academic Standards: Writing Process / Organization and Focus

Materials Needed: 4-5 fiction and nonfiction books about the same topic
colored copy paper (1 per student)
    OR Prompt Attack Template
(yellow) lined paper, pencils

Introduction:
I have brought several books in today. Can anyone tell me what all these books have in common? *They are all about the same topic.* Discuss how books can be very different from one another, but they always focus on the title, or the topic.

Lesson:
If we wanted to write a story about something like a dog, what questions might we want to answer in our story? Put the web on the board and show how question words help to guide the focus and order of the story. If you use the Prompt Attack, read the prompt to students and use prompt questions in the web.

Guided Practice: Brainstorming: (5 minutes) pink brainstorming paper
Keep the pencil moving! Students will create their own webs about a dog as the teacher walks around the room encouraging those students who are not writing. You may encourage them with questions such as: What do you want me to know about this dog? Where do you think the dog lives? How do you care for a dog? Would a dog make a good pet? After five minutes talk about the ideas you have seen in the webs. Tell students they will take this information and start writing a paragraph about a dog.

Conclusion:
What is the most important thing you learned today about writing a paragraph?
All the sentences should be about the topic.
Clip the papers together and collect them.

Assessment:
Informal assessment-teacher observation.
    Did everyone participate?

Reflection:

Lesson Plan: Stick to the Topic Day 2

Title: **Stick to the Topic**   **Minutes: 60 minutes**
Source: *The Simple 6™: A Writing Rubric for Kids*

Behavioral Objectives: Students will:
- share their paragraphs.
- identify sentences that don't belong.
- watch the teacher model exemplary writing.
- role play a piece of a paragraph.
- write the final draft.

Academic Standards: Writing Process / Organization and Focus

Materials Needed: 3 transparencies of sample paragraphs
yesterday's rough drafts
paper for final copy

Introduction:
  Yesterday we learned about sticking to the topic. Who can tell me what that means?

Lesson:
  Show transparencies of sample writing. Discuss. Make sure all students understand what sticking to the topic means.

Guided Practice:
  Students will read their rough drafts silently, making revisions if necessary. Two volunteers will read their stories orally. After each, ask the class, *"Did he stick to the topic?"* Make sure everyone understands the concept. Then divide into groups of three to repeat the process with everyone's story, offering assistance when necessary.
  Students will make the final copy of their story.

Conclusion:
  What is the most important thing you learned today about writing a paragraph?
  All the sentences should be about the topic.

Assessment:
  Informal assessment-teacher observation.
    Did everyone participate in the small group activity?
    Did students stick to the topic in their rough drafts?

Reflection:

Week 2: Logical Order   # Day 1/Thursday

When introducing the idea of logical order, use a familiar book such as <u>The Three Bears.</u> With younger students, begin by reading the story so that everyone has the same version in mind. By retelling a well-known story, students easily get the idea of logical order.

Option 1: Traditional Brainstorming: Review question words on the board. You might use *who, what, when, why* and *where*. Be careful not to list them. Students have the tendency to write their story in the order that you list the question words. Distribute a sheet of brainstorming paper to each student and give them five to eight minutes to write their question words and brainstorm their ideas. (Time it.)

<u>**Organize**</u> At the end of brainstorming time, give students a piece of unlined newsprint that has been folded into thirds. Now, introduce *logical order.* What does logical order mean? If you were to divide this story into three parts, what might you call them? *beginning, middle and end* Label your paper **B, M,** and **E**. This sheet will contain ideas or phrases. Do not start writing your story in sentences yet. (This is very hard for students. Model phrasing for them before you ask them to do it on their own.) Through class discussion come up with the following:

Beginning: porridge too hot
               bears go for walk

Middle: Goldilocks comes in
               eats porridge
               breaks chair
               falls asleep

End: bears come home
               Goldilocks runs away

Check with students to make sure they agree that everything is in the right order. Focus on key words that helped get the events in logical order. Review: Did we stick to the topic?

Pass out (yellow) legal paper. Students will have 15 minutes to write a rough draft. Remind them to write on every other line of the (yellow) paper. At the end of 15 minutes, collect the papers.

Option #2: Prompt Attack

Pose the story of <u>The Three Bears</u> as a prompt.

There was once a little girl named Goldilocks, who broke into the house of the three bears while they were out taking a walk. How did she find the house? What did she do once she got in? Why didn't she leave?

How did she find the house?
_____
_____
*
*

(Three Bears)

Why didn't she leave?
_____
*
*

What did she do once she got in?
_____
*
*

Once students have identified the questions for the body, teach specific strategies for the beginning and end. (Introduction and conclusion strategies are found on the next page.)

Introduction:

At the very lowest level, tell what you are writing about. If you can, start with a lead first.

<u>Long ago there was a girl named Goldilocks.</u>   **Lead**
<u>She was walking in the woods one day when</u>
<u>she noticed three bears going in the other direction.</u>   **Title/Topic**

Conclusion:

Don't just say, "The End"! Lead into your conclusion, getting the reader ready to find out how the story ends. Add your thoughts to the end, if you think it sounds like it needs something else.

<u>Goldilocks ran and ran until she was out of breath.</u> **Lead**
<u>She was safe at last!</u>   **Solution**
<u>She would never do that again!</u>   **Thoughts**

Check with students to make sure they agree that everything is in the right order. Focus on key words and ideas – not complete sentences. Pass out rough draft paper. Students will have 15 minutes to write a draft from their planning page. They should always write their rough draft every other line. Give students a three-minute warning and a "you should be finishing your last sentence" warning. Have students put their writing in the folders and collect them.

Strategies for Inviting Beginnings

Purpose: *to inform the reader of the topic*
to get the reader interested enough to continue reading

| Description | Create a vivid description of the setting, character, background, or mood. It may build up to the introduction of the topic. |

It seemed like an ordinary Tuesday, but I took one look at Mrs. Smith's face and I could just tell something special was going to happen. Sure enough, before lunch she made the big announcement. Our class was going to be in a play!!

Example from literature: _____

| Direct Quotation | Use a speaker to get the reader's attention right away. |

"Come on, Joe! Hurry! You'll be late for the bus!"
I could hear my mom yelling, and I knew the bus would leave without me, but I needed just a few seconds more to reach what I'd hidden under my mattress last night.

Example from literature: _____

| Opinion | Take a stand and support it with substantial reasons. |

I think my teacher, Mrs. Smith, should get the Citizen of the Year Award. I am going to give you many reasons why I think she deserves it.

Example from literature: _____

| Question | Start with a question that will get the reader to start thinking about the topic. |

Did you ever have a teacher that made school so fun that you never wanted to absent?

Example from literature: _____

| Word | Write one word that sets the tone or lets the reader know the topic. |

School. I just can't get enough of it! Why, you wonder, would I like school so much? It's because of my great teacher, Mrs. Smith.

Example from literature: _____

Strategies for Strong Conclusions

Purpose: *to summarize or review*
to solve a problem
to give cause for reflection

Common Conclusions: Fiction

Elaboration   Make sure that your conclusion is more than one sentence.
Eliminate "The End."

The school year is coming to an end, and I will have to say good-bye to Mrs. Smith. I will always remember what a great teacher she was.

Example from literature: _____

Open   Close with a hint of things to come. . .

As the bus pulls away, I look back to see Mrs. Smith talking to a man in a moving van.
Example from literature: _____

Opinion   Strongly restate the stand taken throughout the paper.

I just can't seem to say enough great things about Mrs. Smith. She was truly the best teacher I ever had. If I end up being a teacher, I hope to be just like her.

Example from literature: _____

Question   Close with a question or a series of questions that causes the reader to reflect or create an opinion.

I wonder if Mrs. Smith has ever thought about moving up to the next grade level?

Example from literature: _____

Week 2: Logical Order   Day2/Friday

GREAT IDEA!

Begin the day with a different fairy tale such as <u>Little Red Riding Hood</u> or <u>The Three Little Pigs.</u> Let one student be the beginning, three be the middle, and another be the end. Tell the story in order (one sentence per student). Review strategies for beginnings and endings. The beginning should always tell what you are writing about. The conclusion should tell how the story ends without saying "The End." Ask several different students to come up with and play the part of the beginning and end.

With the **BME** or Prompt Attack template, show students how the planning and organizing would look. This should be done together on the board or overhead projector. Make sure all students understand the importance of planning before writing.

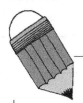

Reminders for Prompt Attack

1. Start with the title or topic of the story and write it in the oval.

2. Use the questions from the prompt for the web.

3. Answer the questions in complete sentences.

4. Add key words for detail ideas next to the *.

5. Start the introduction. At the very least, tell what is being written about.

6. End with more than "The End."

7. Don't spend more than 10-15 minutes on this. Start the rough draft.

During instruction, students may use the template that is provided. On standardized assessments students are typically required to use blank paper.

Pass out yesterday's rough drafts. Give students time to read their stories to themselves. *Does the story make sense? Did it stick to the topic? Does it have a beginning, middle and end?* Make sure students understand that having a beginning, middle and end, and by using works like first, next, then and finally, give the story logical order. If they don't have a strong conclusion can they think of ways to make improvements?

Give students 15 minutes to share their work in a small group and make necessary corrections. Pass out paper for the final draft. Give students time to copy their finished story. Clip all the pieces together and turn them in. Students who want to share their work may post it on the writing bulletin board for everyone to read.

Your ideas:

_____

_____

_____

_____

_____

_____

_____

_____

_____

_____

Week 2: Logical Order   **Follow-up Activities**

* Read subsequent stories throughout the week to the class. Practice breaking down the main events into phrases to be written on the **B M E** Chart or Prompt Attack Template. Let students lead the discussion and write on the board.

* Type the main events of another well-known fairy tale in sentences that are out of order. Have students cut out the sentences and glue them onto another sheet of paper in the correct order.

* Read another fairy tale. Brainstorm and organize together. Write a story as a class. Have all students copy it to practice best handwriting.

* Talk about "How to" paragraphs. Make a peanut butter and jelly sandwich in front of the class. Together, write a paragraph that explains exactly how to do it. Keep asking these questions: Does it make sense? Does it flow? Is everything in the right order? Can you form a clear picture in your mind as you read?

Your ideas

_____

_____

_____

_____

_____

_____

_____

_____

_____

As students get better at putting the events in order, it's important to keep reminding them to have a definite ending to the story. Students miss this part of logical order more than any other, especially the primary students.

Lesson Plan: Logical Order, Day 1

Title: Logical Order   **Minutes: 60 minutes**

Source: *The Simple 6™: A Writing Rubric for Kids*

Behavior Objectives: Students will:
- create a web after listening to a familiar story.
- use the web to organize their thoughts.
- retell the story in the correct order.

Academic Standards: Writing Process / Organization and Focus

Materials Needed: a short version of <u>The Three Bears</u>
colored copy paper (1 per student)
BME (beginning, middle, end paper
   OR Prompt Attack template
yellow lined paper, pencils

Introduction:
   Who knows the story of <u>The Three Bears</u>? If I asked you to tell a very short version of the story, could you do it? What might we use to make the task a little easier? (graphic organizer: BME or Prompt Attack)

Lesson:
   Let's try to rewrite the story of <u>The Three Bears</u> using as few words as possible. We will write them on a beginning, middle and end paper. We are not going to write whole sentences. We will write our ideas down in short phrases. If Prompt Attack is used, follow the reminders on page 55.

Guided Practice:
   Working with the **BME** paper or Prompt Attack template, students will rewrite the story.

   Rough Draft: (10-15 minutes)
   Use yellow lined rough draft paper. *Every other line!*

Conclusion:
   What is the most important thing to remember when you are retelling a story? *Get the events in the right order. Always tell what you are writing about. Finish with more than THE END.*

Assessment: Informal assessment/teacher observation.
                    Did everyone participate?
                    Look over BME papers. Use the information to assess weaknesses,
                    and let it guide the next day's lesson.
Reflection:

Lesson Plan: Logical Order, Day 2

Title: Logical Order   **Minutes: 60 minutes**

Source: *The Simple 6™: A Writing Rubric for Kids*

Behavior Objectives: Students will:
- read their stories to see if they make sense.
- share their work in a small group.
- give suggestions for strong conclusions.
- revise, edit and write final drafts.

Academic Standards: Writing Process / Organization and Focus

Materials Needed: yesterday's work
final draft paper

Introduction:
Yesterday we talked a lot about the story of <u>The Three Bears</u>. Today we're going to arrange the events in another fairy tale.

Lesson:
Who knows the story of <u>Little Red Riding Hood?</u> (Ask for a volunteer to come up to the front and choose 1 **B**, 3 **M**s and an **E**. Let this student lead the discussion.) Remind them to focus on the introduction, three main events, and a conclusion.

Did the **BME** paper help you yesterday? Who would like to come to the board, lead the discussion, and write the phrases onto the **BME** chart? Remember to use as few words as possible. If Prompt Attack was used, follow that format instead.

Guided Practice:
Pass out yesterday's work. Give everyone time to read their rough draft. Did you stick to the topic? Are your events in logical order? Do you have a strong conclusion? If so, you may copy your story on final draft paper.

Conclusion:
What is the most important thing to remember when you get to the end of your story?

Finish with a strong conclusion. Say more than THE END.

Assessment: Informal assessment/teacher observation.
Did everyone participate?
Did everyone respect the student leaders?
How many students needed assistance while doing the final drafts?

Reflection:

Week 3: Interesting Words   Day 1/Thursday
(think Challenging Vocabulary)

Our focus this week is to increase the level of vocabulary used by students in their writing. While we would like to see students use more interesting words while they write their first draft, words are more likely to be exchanged and inserted during revision. The most beneficial strategy for increasing vocabulary is to read more, but here are some simple ideas for students to use as they are introduced to revision.

Strategy #1: Replace generic words.

Show the students two cans of dog food – one generic and one name brand. Ask what the difference is. Generic dog food is ordinary, while brand name dog food is better. Write three generic, or ordinary, words on the board that have been pulled from the generic dog food can.

went	**said**	**big**
traveled	exclaimed	huge
scurried	replied	gigantic

Ask students to think of synonyms for each word. List them beneath the generic words. As students volunteer, have them write the new words on strips of paper that would be put in the appropriate dog food can.

Strategy #2: Replace overused words.

Read through any rough draft or old piece of writing. Listen and look for words that have been used over and over. Highlight them and replace them with new words or phrases. (I like. . .I went. . .I would. . .and then. . .)

Strategy #3: Use words that are specific to the topic.

Think about the assigned topic. Can you think of words that might be relevant to this topic only? They might be words that describe a certain habitat or situation. They might be scientific or historical words. What specific words go with this story? Make a word bank of words that go with this particular topic. Use as many of them as you can in your writing. (Word Bank template on page 67)

Strategy #4: Insert powerful adjectives.

While we think about inserting adjectives to make writing more descriptive, it is also a strategy that can be used here. Choose adjectives carefully, looking at their quality – not quantity.

Ask students to write about a topic that is familiar, is easy to put in order, and has words specific to the topic. Try something like "Getting to School on Time."

Getting to School on Time

Every family has their own routine in the morning. What do you do before you get to school?

Be sure to include:
- Time and place
- Events in order
- Interesting words

Brainstorming: Use Brainstorming Paper (5 minutes)

Organizing: Use **BME** Paper (10 minutes)

} OR Prompt Attack (15 min.)

Rough Draft: Use Yellow Rough Draft paper (15 min.)

Name   Chessia, Grade 4

Morning Routine: BME

B: alarm
wake up
6:30

M: brush teeth
make bed
change clothes
turn on CD
go to kitchen to eat
Mom fixes hair

E: Mom drives me to school

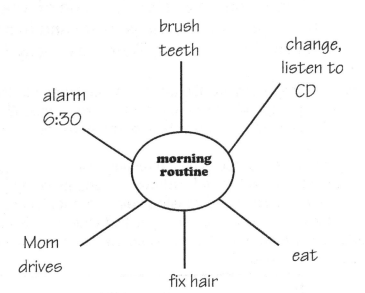

Morning Routine: Chessia's Rough Draft

Every day I wake at 6:30 sharp. I slide down the hall to the bathroom and brush my teeth. I wander back to my room to make my bed. By then it's around 6:55. I turn on a CD and change. I hop into the kitchen and eat. My mom does my hair and then I climb into the car and my mom drives me to school.

Week 3: Using Interesting Vocabulary   Day 2/Friday

Introducing Students to Revising

On the overhead projector or computer screen, show students a completed paragraph that sticks to the topic, has logical order, but uses very generic words.

> Butterflies are flying bugs. The butterfly goes through three stages of life. They are caterpillar, cocoon, and adult. They also have feelers and large wings. They do not make noise. Butterflies are interesting.

Ask for a student volunteer to come up and lead the discussion on how to improve the paragraph by substituting "three brand name words." With a red pen, first identify the words that will be replaced. Then take suggestions for words that might be more interesting. Have students read the revised paragraph together orally. Below is a second example if needed.

> The Monarch Butterfly is one of the many insects. It has three parts to it, wings, body and head. The Monarch Butterfly likes flowers. There are many Monarch Butterflies.

Following each activity, the teacher should come to the front with her own completed revision of the paragraph. Were the same words chosen? Were the same substitution words used? Does it matter? Were both paragraphs more interesting than the first one?

To get students to focus on interesting words, motivate them by helping them to first visualize what they want to write. Showing students some pictures of butterflies and talking about their specific characteristics help students focus on precise language. Generating a Word Bank with words that are specific to the topic is also an excellent motivator for students. Show them the Word Bank below that would have made their revision of the butterfly paragraph much easier.

WORD BANK			
Monarch	colorful	abdomen	caterpillar
beautiful	insect	flyers	quickly
cocoon	head	delicate	detailed
wings	thorax	attracted	deadly

The Word Bank

Before passing out yesterday's rough draft, talk to students about words that might be special to their story. What words might you use in a story about getting ready for school, that you might not use otherwise? List these on the board in a box labeled WORD BANK.

Word Bank			
rush	favorite	cereal	outfit
styles	curls	exciting	relaxing
adventurous		comfortable	

Pass out yesterday's rough draft. Students will be given their own red pen. Again, give students time to read their work. After reading their story they should ask themselves:

Did I **stick to the topic?**
Does the story have **logical order** and a **strong conclusion?**
Can I find three generic words that can be substituted for **interesting words?**

Students should circle at least three different generic words in the rough draft. They may use interesting, more challenging words to replace them or to insert as adjectives. When students are satisfied that this is their best writing, they should recopy the story on final draft paper. (They may want to write their "three brand name words" with their new red pen!)

Chessia's Final Draft

Every day I wake up at 6:30 a.m. sharp. Then I slide down the hall in my socks to the bathroom to brush my teeth. I wander back to my room to make my bed. By then it's around 6:55. I turn on a relaxing CD and change into my school clothes. After that I rush into the kitchen and eat my favorite honey-flavored cereal. My mom curls my hair, and then I climb into her comfortable gold car. She drives me to school to start an adventurous, new day.

Give students a copy of the paragraphs on page 64, and ask them to improve one of the paragraphs. They may use the picture or the Word Bank to help them to substitute or include "three brand name words."

Student Revision #1 (written after seeing several pictures)

Butterflies are beautiful insects with their colors, but that means they are deadly to the other animals that eat them. They start out as a caterpillar, then become a cocoon. Finally, they transform into an adult butterfly. They have antennae, large wings, and a skinny body. Their microscopic feet let them move silently and lightly. Butterflies fascinate me.

Student Revision #2 (written after developing a word bank)

The Monarch butterfly is beautiful and colorful. Butterflies are insects, so they have a head, a thorax and an abdomen. Their small, delicate wings flap quickly, so they are excellent flyers. They are attracted to colorful flowers, so that is where you would most likely find them. There are many kinds of butterflies, but I like the Monarch the best.

Before distributing the rough drafts for yesterday's topic "Getting to School on Time" talk to students about words that might be special to their stories. What words might they use in a story about getting ready for school that they might not use otherwise? List these on the board in a box labeled **WORD BANK**.

Word Bank

_____

_____

© 2009 Pieces of Learning
The Simple 6™ Revised Edition

Lesson Plan: Interesting Words, Day 1

Title: Interesting Words   **Minutes: 60 minutes**

Source: *The Simple 6™ A Writing Rubric for Kids*

Behavioral Objectives: Students will:
  • compare generic to name brand food items
  • relate food comparisons to their writing

Academic Standards: Writing Process / Evaluation and Revision
                              Writing Applications / Varied Word Choices

Materials Needed: two containers of (dog) food (generic and name brand)
                             colored computer paper (1 per student)
                             Beginning, Middle, End paper (newsprint)
                             yellow lined paper, pencils

Introduction:
  Show two cans of dog food – one generic and one name brand. Which is better? Why? Explain four strategies that students can use to increase the level of vocabulary in their writing.

Lesson:
  Today you will be writing a story about getting to school on time. Think about replacing at least three of your generic words.

Guided Practice:
  The teacher will assist those students who need help during brainstorming (5 min.), organizing (10 min.), and writing the rough draft (15 min.).

Conclusion: When the time is up, clip all papers together and collect them.

Assessment:
  Informal assessment-teacher observation.
    Did everyone participate?
    How many students need assistance during independent work time?
    Did everyone complete the rough draft?

Reflection:

Lesson Plan: Interesting Words, Day 2

Title: Interesting Words   **Minutes: 60 minutes**

Source: *The Simple 6 ™: A Writing Rubric for Kids*

Behavioral Objectives: Students will:
- recognize generic words.
- listen as the teacher models exemplary writing.
- create a word bank.
- revise a story to include interesting words.

Academic Standards: Writing Process / Evaluation and Revision
                            Writing Applications / Varied Word Choices

Materials Needed: yesterday's writing
                         final draft paper

Introduction:
Who remembers what we talked about yesterday? *(using more challenging vocabulary in our writing)*. Who would like to come up to the front and lead the class in improving this paragraph? (The students will see a very sparse paragraph about a butterfly. A student leads the discussion and revision.)
I would like you all to listen while I read my paragraph. I revised the same one that you just finished. Listen to see if we used the same words. Continue this discussion.

Lesson:
Today we are going to learn to make a Word Bank. The Word Bank should contain words that are special to your particular story. They will help to make your story more interesting. Use the Word Bank to finish your story about getting to school on time. Think about replacing at least three of your generic words. You will be circling them with your red pen and writing the new word above it in red. When you have revised your story you may recopy it.

Guided Practice:
Students use their red pens to find three generic words and replacing them with three interesting words from their word bank. Give students 10 minutes to do this. They are then given 15 minutes to recopy their story.

Conclusion: When the time is up, clip all papers together and collect them.

Assessment: Informal assessment-teacher observation.
                   Did everyone participate?
                   Could everyone identify and substitute three words?
                   Did everyone complete the final draft on time?

Reflection:

Week 4: Review   Day 1/Thursday

It's time to give students a break from the routine. There will be four writing activities to choose from. Before introducing the activities ask a student to lead the class in a review of what has been talked about so far.

Stick to the Topic

Are all the sentences about the topic?

If questions were given on the prompt, were they answered?

Does the writing make sense?

Logical Order

Is there a beginning? (If so, does the reader know what our story is going to be about?)

Is your body about the answers to the questions in the prompt?

Did you use words like *first, next, then,* and *finally* if they were appropriate?

Do your ideas flow from one to the next in an orderly, understandable way?

Did you finish with a definite, strong conclusion?

Interesting Words

Did you replace at least three generic words with "three brand name words?"

Did you replace words that were used over and over?

Did you think of a list of 10 words that might relate specifically to the topic?

Did you insert any adjectives?

Did you choose precise verbs?

Week 4: Review   Day 1/Thursday

Activity 1:   Write a story from a picture.

Choose one of four magazine pictures on the bulletin board.

Remember to: **Stick to the topic.**

Check for **logical order** and **include a strong conclusion.**

Include **interesting words**

Activity 2:   Add a conclusion.

Here are two stories. Read them both. Did you notice they don't have endings? Choose the one you could best end. Recopy the story. You may draw a picture to go with it.

The Mysterious Substitute by Luke, Grade 3

I couldn't believe what happened the day we had a substitute teacher! It all started when this lady walked into our classroom. She was carrying an unusual sack. It was made of blue cloth, and it had gold stars on it. She hid it under her desk, which made me really want to know what was inside. As I worked quietly at my seat, I heard my friends whispering, "I wonder what's in the sack?" It was just about time for lunch when she put the cloth sack on top of the desk.

Tricky Tale by Katie, Grade 5

Long ago, there was a doctor who had a special ability to talk to animals. His name was Dr. Amazing. One day he was up on a hill when a bird came up to him. She was crying.

Well, the bird must not have known the doctor could talk to animals because she was very surprised when the doctor asked, "What is wrong, my friend?"

"Wow, you can talk to me and understand me!" the bird said. "My name is Carlie, and I'm a cardinal. Back in the Dark Woods my family is wounded, and I came to find help. Could you help me?"

> "Sure," the doctor said, and he followed the bird into the forest.   All of sudden, a fox came upon them. He was limping, so the doctor said, "What's wrong? What can I do for you?"
> "My leg has been hurting all day," the fox said.
> "Why don't I check it out? Asked Dr. Amazing. "Well, it looks like you have a sprained ankle," said the doctor as he bandaged it up.
> The doctor and Carlie the bird moved along the tangled trees and bushes. Soon they came to a spot that was filled with fabulously built nests in extremely tall trees.
> All of a sudden, Carlie shouted to the doctor, "Look at me!"

Activity 3:   Write a story from a Word Bank.

Do the words in these Word Banks remind you of a story? Choose the Word Bank you like the best and use the words to help you write an interesting story. If you would rather make up your own Word Bank, that is also a choice.

I	II	III	IV	V
scientist	admission	download	amphibian	redecorate
gorillas	theatre	program	unusual	video
entertain	projector	message	biologist	casual
behavior	hilarious	rip	observation	entertain
midnight	interruption	text	poisonous	remote
experiment	refreshments	respond	caution	plasma
arrived	assistance	virus	habitat	technology
observe	terrifying	laptop	awesome	comfortable

Activity 4:   Learn about What-Why Prompts

The teacher will show students a What-Why prompt such as:
  What is your favorite month?
  Why do you like it so much?

Students will learn that instead of creating story middles with answers to questions, they now have to come up with three reasons for their choice. The Template for What-Why Prompt Attack and instructions are on the following pages.

Day 2/Friday

Students may continue on their Thursday activity or choose a second activity.

PROMPT ATTACK!

Follow these steps to attack a What/Why Prompt.

Step 1   Start with the title.

Step 2   Answer the What question.
Write it as you would if you were asking yourself.

The answer will most likely become part of your introduction.

Step 3   Add other IDEAS for your introduction.

If you can't think of any, leave blank *** to guide you in the number of sentences you will need in this part of your story.

Step 4   Web Why #1 as its own paragraph.

Step 5   Repeat for Why #2 and Why #3.

Consider using some of the ideas from the prompt for reasons.

Step 6   Use the strategies you know for writing an introduction.

Possibilities: Start with a hook. (might be a question)

Develop a setting OR

write an overview of the reasons you are going to give.

Restate the title or topic.

(Lower level or younger writers might only restate the title.)

Step 7   Use the strategies you know for writing a conclusion.

Possibilities: Lead into the ending.

Review your reasons.

Finish with your feelings, an opinion, or some questions you still wonder about.

Step 8   After about 10-15 minutes, you're ready to start your rough draft.

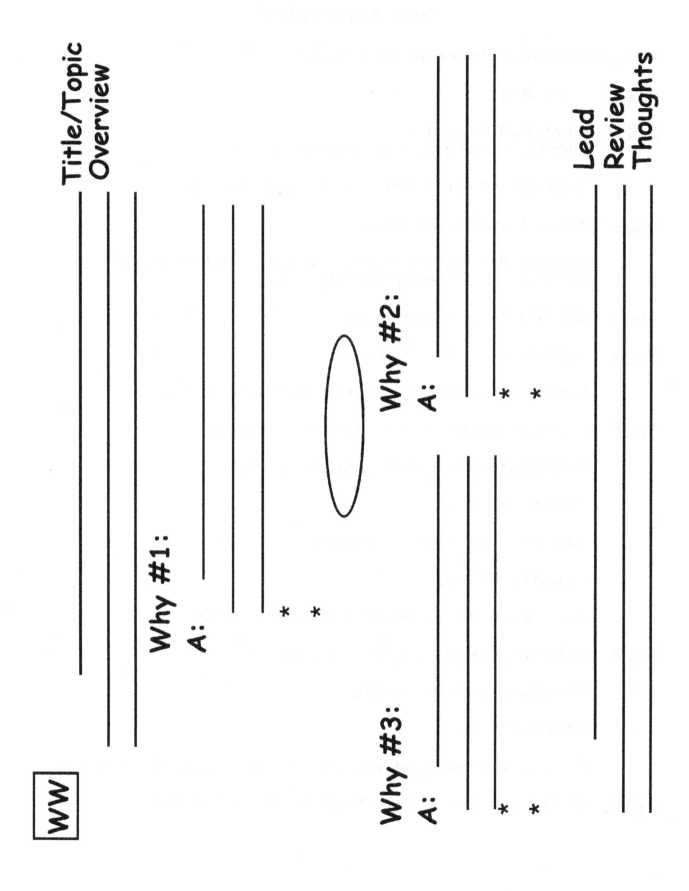

Lesson Plan: Week 4 Review Day 1 and 2

Title: Review: Stick to the Topic   **Minutes: 60 minutes**
                    Logical Order
                    Interesting Words

Source: *The Simple 6™: A Writing Rubric for Kids*

Behavioral Objectives: Students will:
- write a story.
- create or write from a Word Bank.
- make an activity for another group.
- create a graphic organizer

Academic Standards: Writing Process / Organization and Focus, Vocabulary
                            Writing Applications / Varied Word Choices

Materials Needed: magazine pictures, stories without endings, Word Banks,
                            What-Why Prompt Attack template

Introduction:

Who remembers what we have studied so far in writing? This week we will take a break from our usual writing routine. You will get to choose an activity that you would like to do. There will be four choices.

Lesson:

Explain activities 1-4 which are set up in various stations in the classroom. Let students go to the area that interests them.

Guided Practice:

Activity 4 needs the teacher for instruction of Prompt Attack. It is helpful if there is another adult to walk around the room offering suggestions or assistance to those who need it.

Conclusion:

When the time is up, students will collect all their work so they can return to it the next day.

Assessment:

Informal assessment-teacher observation.
   Did everyone participate enthusiastically?
   Did they respect each other's writing time by working quietly?
   Did each student complete one of the activities?

Celebrate student success by taking pictures as they work today. Use the pictures to enhance your writing bulletin board or your school newspaper.

Reflection:

Week 5: Different Sentence Patterns   Day 1/Thursday

Students have now been introduced to half of the components of *The Simple 6™:* sticking to the topic, writing ideas in logical order, and using interesting words. They have reached the point that divides a non-passing (Score 3) from a passing paper (Score 4). The fourth point is critical, but it can be presented in a non-threatening, "I've Got a Secret" kind of way.

If the story still sounds like a list, it doesn't pass. So to keep writing from having a list-like quality, encourage students to write various types of sentences. Being able to change sentence patterns takes student writing to another level. While it is definitely a developmental skill, there are ways even young students can be made aware of strategies that can offer variety to their sentence patterns. The six strategies that seem to be easiest for elementary students are:

- including questions, especially at the beginning or end
- listing a series of ideas in one sentence
- combining short sentences to make a compound sentence
- improving sentence beginnings by adding adverbs or prepositional phrases
- using direct quotations so that characters have more personal interaction
- changing the order of the words in the sentence

Consider integrating this week's topic with science or social studies. Throughout the week, keep a list of facts that you have learned in one of the content areas. (If you have extra board space, it's good to keep an accumulative list there so everyone is reminded of these facts as the week progresses.) These facts will become the body of their paragraphs and will make a perfect example for changing sentence patterns.

On Thursday, ask students what they have been studying in a content area. Turn this information into a topic sentence, and write it on the board. Ask them how they feel about this unit, and help them come up with a general concluding sentence that combines fact with feelings. Leaving an open space for the middle, write the concluding sentence on the board. Give students a sheet of rough draft paper, and remind them to write on every other line. Ask them to copy the topic sentence from the board. When everyone has finished, ask students to look at the list of facts on the board (read them together with younger students) and write three middle, or detail, sentences about the topic. End with the concluding sentence that is already on the board. Give students about five minutes to do this independently (or you can do it together on the board). Most students will provide you with a nice list of facts with almost every sentence starting with the name of the topic.

In this paragraph about birds, students were given the topic sentence and the conclusion. They were asked to volunteer sentences telling factual information that they had learned in science about birds. These sentences were written on the board as the group developed a paragraph they liked. Here's what a group of seven-year-olds created:

> Birds are vertebrates, which means they have backbones. Birds come in all sizes. Birds have colorful feathers and two legs. Birds have beaks, but they have no teeth. Birds build nests for their babies. Some birds stay in their homes. Other birds migrate to warm places. Birds are interesting.

After talking about changing word order, using pronouns, and combining ideas here's how they improved the detail sentences.

> Birds are vertebrates, which means they have backbones. Birds have colorful feathers, two legs, and wings for flying. They can be as small as a peanut or larger than a man! Birds build nests for their babies, and the parents take care of them for a few months. Some bird families stay in their homes, but others migrate to warm places. Birds are interesting.

After reading the paragraph together orally, students were asked if changing one of the statements into a question might make it more interesting. They all agreed that this would work best in the topic sentence or the conclusion. The final paragraph, written by the class, turned out like this:

> Birds are vertebrates, which means they have backbones. Most birds have colorful feathers, two legs, and wings for flying. They can be as small as a peanut or larger than a man! Birds build nests for their babies, and the parents take care of them for a few months. Some bird families stay in their homes, but others migrate to warm places. Aren't birds interesting?

Students were then able to go back to their own paragraphs and make necessary changes that would give their sentences variety and make their paragraphs more interesting.

When they finished, they were given a mini-rubric that had only the first four points of *The Simple 6™* on it. All students whose writing stuck to the topic, had logical order, interesting words, and varied sentence patterns had just entered **"the passing zone!"**

Week 5: Different Sentence Patterns   Friday/Day 2

Start the lesson by grouping students in fours. They will work together to revise a story. This *revision* team works together to make improvements in a piece of writing. If you have an overhead projector for each group, this will make the exercise more fun for students.

Always start the new lesson with a review of what has been learned so far. Remind students that **changing word order** will improve sentence fluency. **Combining short sentences** will eliminate choppiness. **Adding a question** or starting with a **prepositional phrase** will create interest. The main idea is to get students to recognize and be able to improve writing that has a list-like quality.

Provide students with a topic and a new list of facts on the board. (This may be something they studied earlier in the year, but they must be familiar with the topic.) Go through the list together. Ask if they have ideas for a great topic sentence. *How many of them can think of at least three supporting detail sentences? What about a conclusion?* When you are satisfied that everyone has some ideas, tell them they are going to look at a paragraph that is already finished but that you think can be improved by varying the sentence patterns. Remind students that this is something they have already studied, so you know they will have lots of interesting ideas.

Give each group of students the same transparency to work from. As a group, they will make changes in sentence patterns to create interest in their factual paragraphs. Give them five to ten minutes to accomplish the task. Then have each group read their improved paragraph and discuss it with the rest of the class. Each group should ask if there are any questions from the other students in the class.

When you are satisfied that each revision group clearly understands how to improve the paragraph by changing sentence patterns, ask the groups to divide in half. Tell the students they will now be working with a partner to revise a factual paragraph. In addition to varying the sentence patterns, they must also ask and answer all the questions on the rubric that have been studied so far:

- Does the paragraph **stick to the topic?**
- Does it have **logical order** (and an especially strong conclusion)?
- Are there at least **three challenging words?**
- Do **different sentence patterns** make the writing more interesting?

The partners will work together to make corrections on a paper copy of the paragraph. Students can recopy paragraphs or use computers where the original version has been saved. They then make their revisions on the computer and re-save to the disk. After writing both student names on the piece, have them print a hard copy, and turn it in for posting on the writing board. This might also be a great opportunity to invite your principal into class. Students can give a short review of what they have learned so far, stories can be shared, and students can impress the principal with what has been accomplished in five weeks!

Week 5: Different Sentence Patterns   Follow-Up Activities

* Cut pictures out of magazines and laminate them to index cards or large card stock. Put a Fact List on the back that gives students background information to write from.

* Write several letters, and put each one in a separate envelope. Let students choose an envelope. They may either rewrite the letter, eliminating the list-like quality that it has, or they may choose to answer the letter, making sure they vary the sentence patterns in their response.

* Write three general knowledge questions on a card. Students will answer the three questions, but each response must be structured differently.

Your ideas

_____

_____

_____

_____

_____

_____

_____

_____

_____

_____

Sample Fact List from a Content Unit

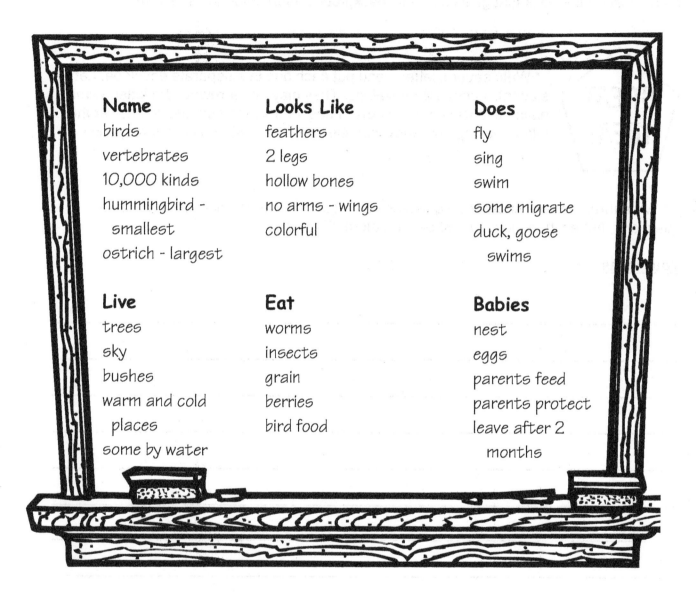

Name
birds
vertebrates
10,000 kinds
hummingbird -
   smallest
ostrich - largest

Looks Like
feathers
2 legs
hollow bones
no arms - wings
colorful

Does
fly
sing
swim
some migrate
duck, goose
   swims

Live
trees
sky
bushes
warm and cold
   places
some by water

Eat
worms
insects
grain
berries
bird food

Babies
nest
eggs
parents feed
parents protect
leave after 2
   months

Lesson Plan: Different Sentence Patterns Day 1

Title: **Different Sentence Patterns**   **Minutes: 60 minutes**
Source: *The Simple 6™: A Writing Rubric for Kids*

Behavioral Objectives: **Students will:**
- create new sentences by changing word order.
- develop a paragraph in a large group.
- use information they learned in a content area.

Academic Standards: Writing Process / Organization and Focus
Writing Applications / Evaluation & Revision
Writing Conventions / Sentence Structure

Materials Needed: a list of science or social studies facts from current unit
(yellow) lined paper, pencils

Introduction:
We have been making a list of (science) facts on the board all week. Today we are going to use them to write a descriptive paragraph.

Lesson:
Let's start by naming the topic we have been studying about in (science) and turning that idea into a topic sentence. Write the topic sentence at the top of the board. Skipping space for the middle, write a conclusion at the bottom. Explain to students that the conclusion restates the general idea of the story, may include feelings, and may also be stated as a question that will encourage the reader to learn more facts about the topic. Review the list of facts on the board to use to write the detail sentences. Students will have 5-10 minutes to write three detail sentences.

Guided Practice:
Working from their individual paragraphs, students complete the group paragraph on the board. Then they will improve their writing by changing the word order of their own detail sentences. Students may also replace a statement with a question if it is appropriate in their pieces. Do this activity together on the board as students review their individual pieces. Have students copy the final paragraphs from the board or revise their own.

Conclusion:
What did you learn today about keeping your sentences from sounding like a list of facts? *Use a variety of sentence patterns. Who can tell me some strategies for changing sentence patterns that we have worked on during mini-lessons? Insert a question, change word order, combine short sentences, write sentences with commas in a series.*

Assessment:
Informal assessment-teacher observation.
Did everyone participate?
Read student paragraphs. Have they lost their list-like qualities?
Tally this week's papers: PASS/NOT PASS

Reflection:

Lesson Plan: Different Sentence Patterns Day 2

Title: Different Sentence Patterns   **Minutes: 60 minutes**
Source: *The Simple 6™: A Writing Rubric for Kids*

Behavioral Objectives: **Students will:**
- create new sentences by changing word order.
- use factual information learned in a content area.
- revise a paragraph with a small group/partner.

Academic Standards: Writing Process / Evaluation and Revision
Writing Conventions / Sentence Structure

Materials Needed: a list of science or social studies facts from current unit
4 or 5 overhead projectors with paragraph on transparency
paper copies of another, content-based paragraph

Introduction:
   Today we are going to work on improving our writing by varying the sentence patterns. Before we do that, though, who can remember all the parts of the rubric we have learned so far? (*Stick to the topic, Logical order, Interesting words, Different sentence patterns*) *Who would like to come up to the front and lead the discussion?*

Lesson:
   You are going to be working in groups to revise a piece of writing. We are going to be using a topic that we have already studied so I know you already have many facts in your head. Who remembers how we began this process yesterday? *Topic sentence, conclusion, then details. When we finished we examined the detail sentences to make sure they didn't sound like a list.*

Guided Practice:
   Each group will work together to revise a paragraph on the overhead projector. Working from their transparencies and fact lists, students will improve the paragraph by changing the word order in their sentences, combining short sentences to form compound sentences, or by using commas in a series. Students may also replace a statement with a question if it is appropriate in their piece.

Conclusion:
   What did you learn today about keeping your sentences from sounding like a list of facts? *Use a variety of sentence patterns. Who can tell me some strategies for changing sentence patterns? Change word order, insert a question, combine short sentences, use commas in a series, etc.*

Assessment:
   Informal assessment-teacher observation.
      Did everyone participate?
      Each group will read their paragraphs to the rest of the class.
      Have they lost their list-like qualities?

Reflection:

Week 6: Descriptive Sentences   **Thursday/Day 1**

Descriptive writing is nothing more than getting the picture you have in your head down onto the paper so the reader sees the same thing. There are many ways to accomplish this, but there are four very simple strategies that students can use to guide them. Tell students to close their eyes and picture this sentence.

Last night I went to the store.

Does everyone have a picture in mind? Can you imagine me going into the store?

After you're sure they can all see you, start the strategies to increase descriptions.

Strategy #1: Include precise verbs. *How did you get there?*

Last night I was chased into the store.

Strategy #2: Include proper nouns. *What's the name of the store?*

Last night I was chased into Jim's Supermarket.

Strategy #3: Insert powerful adjectives. *What kind, which one, how many?*

Last night I was chased into Jim's Supermarket by a vicious dog!

Strategy #4: Add more details. *What did the dog look like?*

Last night I was chased into Jim's Supermarket by a vicious dog! It was a huge German Shepherd with wild eyes and huge, sharp teeth!

Strategy #5: Appeal to the reader's senses. *What literary techniques can be used?*

Last night I was chased into Jim's Supermarket by a vicious dog! It was a huge German Shepherd with wild eyes and huge, sharp teeth! I was so scared I could hear my heart beating right through my shirt!

Teaching students to write descriptively is an ongoing process. This is where age and developmental level play an important role in the decisions you will make regarding the appropriateness of the instruction and activities. Use the standards at each particular grade level to guide the types of literary techniques that will be taught. Because learning to write descriptively takes students to a new level, it is the perfect place for the teacher to model her thought processes. Read the following descriptive paragraph to the class.

> I'll never forget the first snow last year. It was a beautiful, sunny Saturday but the air was crisp. Feeling kind of lazy, I was peacefully reading a Nancy Drew mystery. Suddenly, I caught a glimpse of snow outside my bedroom window. I couldn't resist putting on my heavy coat and going outside. As the first flakes softly brushed my cheeks, I broke into a huge smile. Don't you just love winter?

Ask students what they think of the paragraph. Do they recognize it as descriptive and interesting? What makes it appealing? What strategies were used that they already know about? Review the components of the rubric that have already been learned. Ask the questions:

- Does this paragraph **stick to the topic**?
- Does it have **logical order** and a strong conclusion?
- Did you recognize **interesting vocabulary**?
- Are there **different sentence patterns**, or does the story sound like a list?
- Were the **sentences descriptive?** Did they appeal to your senses?
- What does that mean?

Then read this non-descriptive paragraph to the class.

> I'll never forget the first time it snowed last year. It was sunny, but it was cold out. I felt lazy so I stayed inside to read a book. I looked outside and saw some snowflakes, so I decided to go outside. The snow hit my face, and I was so happy. Don't you love winter?

© 2009 Pieces of Learning
The Simple 6™ Revised Edition

Engage students in a discussion about how the two compare and what strategies were used to make the first paragraph much more interesting than the second one. Focus on and encourage students to talk about *u*sing questions, changing word order, naming characters, and writing compound and complex sentences. Talk about appealing to the senses so the reader actually feels that he is there.

This week give students a copy of their writing samples from earlier in the year. They will be amazed at how much progress they have made! Using their first writing sample as a guide, students will improve their pieces by writing descriptive sentences. They will pay attention to strategies such as naming and describing characters in detail, appealing to their senses to make the reader believe he is "there,"and varying sentence patterns by asking a question, changing word order, using commas in a series, or combining short sentences.

Students will have 30 minutes to revise and write their new rough drafts on (yellow) legal paper. When they are finished, have them clip the original stories to the new rough drafts and turn them in. The original writing samples will remain in progress folders.

Week 6: Descriptive Sentences

Day 2/Friday

Ask for a student volunteer to come forward to lead the class in reviewing the points of the rubric studied so far. Use the Quick Reference Guide on page 28. Remember: The student leader is the only one using the guide. All others are reciting from memory.

Start the lesson by reminding students that there are strategies they can use to be more descriptive writers. As students recall each one, write them on the board.

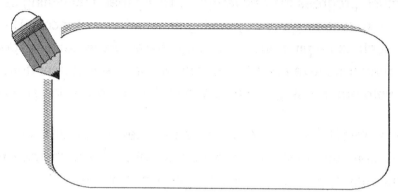

Give students a few minutes to work with a partner to improve another sentence.

Tomorrow I will be good.

or

Then we went home.

Call on pairs to read their sentences. Make sure all students understand the strategies for descriptive writing.

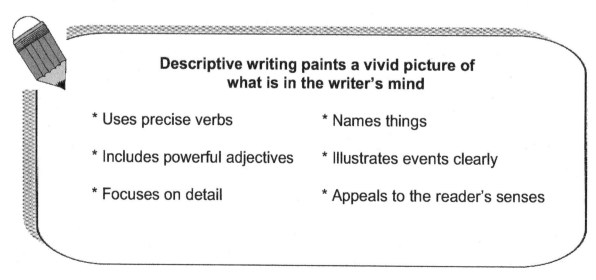

Descriptive writing paints a vivid picture of what is in the writer's mind

* Uses precise verbs

* Includes powerful adjectives

* Focuses on detail

* Names things

* Illustrates events clearly

* Appeals to the reader's senses

Now give students an opportunity to share what they wrote yesterday. After some discussion provide students with a non-descriptive paragraph on the overhead and invite one student to lead the class in improving the sentence quality. Before you begin, remind students that descriptive writing focuses on details that appeal to their reader's senses. It also contains adjectives and precise language.

Sample non-descriptive paragraph

I love cake. It is my favorite. I like it best when my mom bakes. It is so good. I wish I had cake every day.

Other Examples

_____

_____

_____

_____

_____

_____

_____

_____

_____

_____

_____

_____

_____

_____

Week 6: Descriptive Sentences

Follow-up Activities

* Warm-up Activity: Play **"How hot was it?"** Call on several students to answer "It was so hot that . . ." Vary the question each day. "How big was it? How old was it? How scary was it?"

* Cut out a series of pictures from magazines, and write a simple sentence to go with each picture. Post these pictures on a writing bulletin board. Have students write descriptive sentences for each picture, adding them to the bulletin board for other students to read. See which picture gets the most descriptive sentences.

* Play **Sentence Baseball**. Students are divided into teams and assigned positions. The pitcher pitches a topic to the batter. The batter gives a sentence. If the sentence is descriptive, he takes a base. If not, he's out. The teacher is the umpire until students get the hang of it. Then there may be a group of three umpires who decide together.

* Take students on a field trip, outside, into the closet, into a classroom of another grade level, into the principal's office, into the custodians workroom – any place that will give them a change in their usual surroundings. Tell them you are going to this place for five minutes. They may not talk, but they must be very observant. They must pay attention to their senses. How do they feel? What do they see? How does it smell? Did they hear anything unusual? This is especially effective if you can take them outside when there is an abrupt change in the weather.

* Give students a food item such as a slice of apple, a pickle, a Sweet Tart®, a chocolate chip, etc. Have them write a detailed description of the experience.

Your Ideas:

_____

_____

_____

_____

_____

Lesson Plan: Descriptive Sentences Day 1

Title: **Descriptive Sentences**   **Minutes: 60 minutes**
Source: *The Simple 6™: A Writing Rubric for Kids*

Behavioral Objectives: Students will create new sentences using strategies for
                              descriptive writers.

Academic Standards: Writing Process / Evaluation and Revision
                           Writing Applications / Narratives using Sensory Details

Materials Needed: Writing Samples from Week 1
                         Teacher Writing Samples

Introduction:
   Each week our writing is improving because you are learning to organize your thoughts
and show your reader what you see in your mind. Today we will learn more strategies for
writing descriptively. Listen to this sentence. Last night I went to the store. (Proceed with
the five strategies.)

Lesson:
   Listen while I read this story to you. *Read a descriptive paragraph.* Who would like to
share their thoughts about this paragraph? *Choose two or three only.* Now listen to this
(non-descriptive) paragraph. Let's compare the two.
   Which did you like better? Which gave you a clearer picture? Which made you feel like
you were there?

Guided Practice:
   Students will read their writings from Week 1. They will improve the pieces by writing descriptive sentences and applying other revision techniques they have learned.

Conclusion:
   How has your writing improved since the first week?

Assessment:
      Informal assessment-teacher observation.
         Did everyone participate?
         Read student paragraphs. Have they lost their list-like qualities?
         Are sentences descriptive?
      Identify students who are still struggling and make a note to conference with them early
      the following week.
      Put up a BEFORE/AFTER display. Invite students to post their work.

Reflection:

Lesson Plan: Descriptive Sentences Day 2

Title: **Descriptive Sentences**   **Minutes: 60 minutes**
Source: *The Simple 6™: A Writing Rubric for Kids*

Behavioral Objectives: **Students will:**
- appeal to their senses as they write.
- insert adjectives.
- name and describe characters in vivid detail.

Academic Standards: Writing Process / Evaluation and Revision
Writing Applications / Writing Narratives with Sensory Details

Materials Needed: non-descriptive paragraph transparency
yesterday's stories

Introduction: Review. What is descriptive writing?

Lesson:
  Would anyone like to share what they wrote yesterday? Let a few share and invite others to post their BEFORE/AFTER pieces on the bulletin board.
  Here is a paragraph for us to read and improve (overhead). Who would like to lead this activity?

Guided Practice:
  Students will read their works silently from the day before. They will focus on making them as descriptive as possible before copying the final draft.

Conclusion:
  What did you learn this week about making your sentences descriptive? Why is that important?
  After students have completed this assignment, type a sample list of descriptive sentences from this assignment (hopefully one per student). Cut them apart and post them on the writing bulletin board or tape them to your classroom door with stars on them that say "We are Descriptive Writers!!"

Assessment:
  Informal assessment-teacher observation.
    Did everyone participate?
    Read student paragraphs. Have they lost their list-like qualities?
    Did all student writing contain at least one descriptive sentence?
    Have all students had an opportunity to lead the discussion?

Reflection:

Week 7: Writing for an Audience   Day 1 Thursday

Choose a student to review the components using The Simple 6™ Quick Reference Chart. Students should have them memorized by now.

Writing for an audience simply means this:

Was the tone appropriate for the prompt? Does the reader get the feeling you are communicating directly with him? Does your voice or personality shine through your writing?

After introducing the basic concept of **audience** students have a tendency to start their work with, *"Hi. My name is . . ."* Try to discourage this by having them think of an engaging question that might get the reader's attention such as *"Have you ever wondered why volcanoes erupt?"* or *"Have you ever met my oldest sister?"* This technique easily engages the reader. By the same token, endings that say "That's my story. I hope you liked it." need to focus on the writer's emotion or another question related to the topic.

To illustrate the concept of **audience,** change the format for the lesson again. Today, show a series of commercials you have taped in advance. Not only will the topic of **persuasion** be addressed, but students will also realize that the actor (or voice) is talking directly to them – getting a message across that is specifically related to and appropriate for the topic.

Being able to convey emotion and personal feelings is really what writing for an audience is all about. Engage students in *"I Say – You Say"*. I say: *"This turkey is very tasty."* You say: *"I haven't had turkey this delicious since last Thanksgiving at my Grandma's house!"* I say: *"I'm tired."* You say: *"I'm so tired I could fall asleep in this chair!"* Once students get the idea, have them think about the language and expression they use when they are writing a note to a friend. The same is true for talking on the telephone. Role play a short telephone conversation about being invited to a party to illustrate this point. The enthusiasm of the teacher plays an important role in the understanding of this point. The more drama you can bring to this lesson, the better.

GREAT IDEA!

Students should now be ready to write. Writing with emotions such as sadness, embarrassment, fear, excitement, wonder, or profound happiness are safe places to start. Choose topics that lend themselves to the expression of feelings. Give students five minutes for a free write. Do not collect the work this time. Let students file it and share the next day if they choose. Be aware that many students may not want to share work that expresses their feelings about personal topics. Suggest topics like *The Worst School Lunch* or *The Day I Won the Lottery.* Then suggest topics such as *My Best Birthday* or *My Most Embarrassing Moment.*

After students have practiced writing to their emotions, insert topics at a more sophisticated level that address writing with authority, persuasion, or a unique perspective. Some topic ideas might be *If I were President, Making Summer Vacation Longer, Why Reading is Important, My Contribution to the World, etc.*

Remind students to pay more attention during commercials. Ask them to keep a log of commercials they watch. Ask them to categorize them into groups naming different ways the viewers were being persuaded to buy the product. (humor, seriousness, straight facts, a jingle, music, technological/graphic interest, etc.) These ideas can be springboards for other writing activities.

Writing for a specific audience allows students to be themselves, to present their thoughts with originality and in their own voice. The choice of words or phrases they use to make the connection with the audience determines their individual style. When introducing students to the concepts of audience, voice, and style, it is important to remind them: Don't be afraid to write with emotion and personality, but remember the tone the writer takes with the audience has to match the prompt.

Week 7: Audience   # Day 2/Friday

One of the easiest ways to motivate students to write to an audience is to assign them letter writing. Writing to a close friend lends itself to the writer, unveiling his personality because of the familiarity of the reader. By combining letter writing with the excitement of the commercial activity yesterday, ask students to write a letter to their best friend. In the letter they will discuss a new product they have just learned about in a commercial and try to persuade their friend to buy the product. Using a movie preview is also motivating.

Before students start on their letters, have them write one with you. This is an effective activity if done on the overhead/computer screen. Choose a student to be the writer/typist, get everyone's feedback, and send the letter/email. This gives that last bit of encouragement and reinforcement to the student who still doesn't have a feeling for audience and writing with emotion or personality.

Include a poster with this project. Students write the letter and say, *"I'm also enclosing a picture of myself showing you the product. I can't wait until you try it!"* If students are sending their letters by email, scan posters and send as attachments. You might also consider taking digital pictures of the student holding the product. Send those as attachments. Posting letters and pictures on the bulletin board gives everyone an opportunity to share. If students are really enthusiastic about this project, they may want to stage their pictures with costumes and props or make short videos. Don't hesitate to carry this activity over to the following week.

Week 7: Audience   Follow-up Activities

* Write a **commercial** script for a product. Talk directly to your audience.

* Read copies of **speeches** by Martin Luther King, former presidents, recipients of awards (the Emmy's, the Academy Awards, the Country Music Awards, etc.) Compare their tone and style.

* Laminate copies of newspaper **editorials** written by local citizens. Identify sentences in which the author effectively communicated with a specific audience. If the author didn't communicate effectively, rewrite the letter to show how she could have been more persuasive or more connected to the reader.

* Send an **email** to a friend persuading them to read a great book you just finished.

Your ideas:

_____

_____

_____

_____

_____

_____

_____

_____

_____

_____

Lesson Plan: Audience Day 1

Title: Audience   **Minutes: 60 minutes**
Source: *The Simple 6™: A Writing Rubric for Kids*

Behavioral Objectives: Students will recognize style and persuasion in commercials

Academic Standards: Writing Applications / Specific Audience
Style or Voice
Persuasive Composition

Materials Needed: pre-taped commercials (showing a variety of style)
Examples: fast food, auto sales, political campaign,
health-related pitches, upcoming events

Introduction:

Today we are going to watch a series of commercials. I want you to pay attention to the method being used to get your attention. Does the actor speak with emotion? Does it matter that you don't usually see the person speaking? Is there a style to this commercial? Take notes as you watch.

Lesson:

When we write we want to try to connect with the reader just as an actor (or speaker) connects with a viewer during a commercial –with style and voice. We are going to watch a few of the commercials again, and this time I want you to write a sentence from each one that had style or voice. (*Pick Enterprise® . . and we'll pick you up! Not everything can be as good as the original, but Diet Dr. Pepper® is. Great product . . . great warranty, great deals – Jeep®. Zoom, zoom, zoom . . . Mazda®.*) It showed emotion, it was catchy, or there was a certain flair about it that caught your attention. Discuss as a class.

We are going to practice speaking with style by playing *"I say – You say."* Use examples until you are sure everyone has caught on.

Guided Practice:

We are going to do a five-minute "free write" today. You will have five minutes to write a paragraph that expresses one of the following emotions: sadness, embarrassment, fear, excitement, or happiness. These will not be collected. You may share tomorrow if you choose.

Conclusion:

What did you learn today about style and voice? As you watch TV tonight view the commercials from a different perspective. Pay attention to style and voice. You will be using what you learn tomorrow in class.

Assessment: Informal assessment-teacher observation.
Did everyone participate?

Reflection:

Lesson Plan: Audience Day 2

Title: Audience   **Minutes: 60 minutes**
Source: *The Simple 6™: A Writing Rubric for Kids*

Behavioral Objectives: **Students will:**
• write a letter to their best friend.
• persuade a friend to buy a product.

Academic Standards: Writing Applications: Persuasive Composition
Friendly Letter   Specific Audience

Materials Needed: paper or computer

Introduction:
  We have been watching and talking about commercials and how the voice totally focuses on viewers to get their attention and persuade. *To really get students' attention, videotape yourself and play this lesson introduction on a TV. Be very enthusiastic and persuasive!*

Lesson:
  Today you will be writing a letter to your best friend. In the letter you will try to persuade your friend to buy a new product you just saw on a commercial or go to a movie you have just seen.
  The commercial I saw last night that caught my attention was one about _____.
I am going to email my best friend and tell her about this product. You can all help.

Guided Practice:
  When your letter is finished you can draw a poster or take a digital picture of yourself holding the product. Send the letter by email or snail mail – your choice.

Conclusion:
  What did you learn today about connecting with your audience?

Assessment:
  Informal assessment-teacher observation.
    Did everyone participate?
    Read student letters. Can you feel their personality, and are you beginning to see personal style in the students' writing?
    Are they writing with emotion?

Reflection:

Week 8: Peer Scoring and Revision   Day 1/Thursday

By this time students have several pieces of completed writing in their folders. They have had an opportunity to learn the individual components of *The Simple 6™*. Once again, start with a student review of all six components.

Stick to the topic.
Check for logical order.
Include interesting words.
Use different sentence patterns.
Write descriptive sentences.
Write for an audience.

Now it's time to see how this knowledge affects assessment. Students are ready to reverse their roles and learn to be scorers. As a team they will examine a piece of writing, learn how to assign it points, and offer suggestions for improvement.

This is the perfect time to look at anchor papers, which can be downloaded from most state departments of education. Your school system may also have detailed guidelines and writing pieces for you to review with your students. These anchor papers and their explanations further clarify the strategies and ideas behind *The Simple 6™*.

Always start with examples of the best writing first. Talk about what it takes to get a Score 6. Discuss the criteria first; then read and discuss the anchor paper to show the justification for each point. It is always important to mention (not emphasize) the fact that a Score 6 is reserved for papers that are far beyond the expectation. From a student's perspective a Score 5 would be an A, while a Score 6 would be an A+. Keep your expectations high, though, and make your students believe that they can get a Score 6, because it **is** possible.

The Simple 6™
A Writing Rubric for Kids

0/1

____ Stick to the Topic
____ Logical Order
____ Interesting Words
____ Different Sentence Patterns
____ Descriptive Sentences
____ Audience

____ TOTAL POINTS

©Kay Davidson 2004

The Simple 6™
A Writing Rubric for Kids

0/1

____ Stick to the Topic
____ Logical Order
____ Interesting Words
____ Different Sentence Patterns
____ Descriptive Sentences
____ Audience

____ TOTAL POINTS

©Kay Davidson 2004

The Simple 6™
A Writing Rubric for Kids

0/1

____ Stick to the Topic
____ Logical Order
____ Interesting Words
____ Different Sentence Patterns
____ Descriptive Sentences
____ Audience

____ TOTAL POINTS

©Kay Davidson 2004

The Simple 6™
A Writing Rubric for Kids

0/1

____ Stick to the Topic
____ Logical Order
____ Interesting Words
____ Different Sentence Patterns
____ Descriptive Sentences
____ Audience

____ TOTAL POINTS

©Kay Davidson 2004

Anchor Papers

The following anchor papers are student-generated pieces of writing that have been scored using **The Simple 6**™. They help teachers get an idea of the standard set at each level of the rubric. Attaching mini-rubrics (page 98) to each piece makes it easy for teachers as well as students to document progress.

Writing Prompt

Primary Grades

The Lemonade Stand

You and your friends need to make some money, so you decide to have a lemonade stand. Where will you have it? How much will you sell your lemonade for? Who will come? Will you make any money?

Score 6

The Christmas Lemonade Stand

Dylan Brittnay Joe and I were so sad. We didn't have any money to by Christmas presents. Brittnay said, "Let's make lemanade."

Joe said, "that's crazy!"

Dyland said, "it's worth a try."

The price was 30 cents.

We set up our lemanade stand outside but it was so freezing cold that our lemonade got frozen!

I said, "I know what these are! They're snow cones!"

We changed the sine and a lot of people came. Finally we had money for Christmas.

Analysis: This is an excellent story for a beginning writer. It definitely sticks to the topic and has a logical progression, including a strong conclusion. The writer includes words like *lemanade, crazy, frozen,* and *finally it was so freezing cold that our . . .* gets the point for descriptive sentences. This young writer made a connection with the reader when she says *. . . were so sad . . .* and *They're snow cones!*

Score 5

The Tasty Lemonad Stand

One day I was sitting outside. My neighbor looked sad. I went over there and said, "What's wrong?"

My cousins birthday is tomorrow and I haven't earned enough money. I can't go to his birthday party because I don't have a present."

"I will help you Niki," I said. We will make a lemonade stand by the curb.

We got lemonade, cups, and ice. It was 25 cents each. We made $7.25. Niki had money to buy a present and I had a fun time with my friend.

Analysis: This piece has all the points except audience. It definitely sticks to the topic and follows a logical progression with a strong conclusion. Vocabulary beyond the first and second grade level would be *neighbor, cousins, earned,* and *curb*. Different sentence patterns include three compound sentences, a question, and many direct quotations. Descriptive sentences include phrases such as ... *looked sad ... cousins birthday ... lemonade stand by the curb ... made $7.25*. This is a great piece for a seven-year-old student.

The Funny Lemonade Stand   Score 4

One day I was sitting with my friend Abbie. I got an idea! We can have a Lemonade sale. We need $90 to buy our dads a present. I will get the old wood out of our garaj and you will get nails. Then the stand was done. Nobody came. This is my worst enemy! Finally someone came. Then another, then more and there was 10, 230 people here. Oh no! There is a BIG problem. We are out of lemons. Then somebody who was nice gave us some more. We went home at the end.

Analysis: The piece on page 90, The Funny Lemonade Stand, gets a Score 4 for sticking to the topic, even though the verb tenses change throughout the story. There is definitely a beginning, middle, (with an added problem) and end. The piece does not get a point for interesting words, but the sentences are descriptive. The writer speaks to the audience with . . . *I got an idea!* . . . *This is my worst enemy!* . . . *Oh no! There is a BIG problem* . . .

The Best Lemonade Stand   Score 3

One day my friend Ashley and me had a clubhouse. But it fell down. We didn't have enough pieces or enough money to fix it. So Ashley got an idea. We were going to have a lemonade stand. We set up the table. We got cups, and lemonade from my mom. Adults and children came. We had a fun time, we can rebuild the clubhouse.

Analysis: The piece sticks to the topic and has logical order. Interesting words are *clubhouse, pieces, adults,* and *rebuild*. Sentences are not descriptive, and there are not different sentence patterns. Almost all sentences begin with "we." Audience is not attempted.

My Delicious Lemonade Stand   Score 2

The lemonade tasty good, morn thin good. It's delicious.
Next a lot of pepol cama log and the stant is wite I'm with my
friend PJ. He is 6 year old. I am eaat year old. Then aveyone
wint inside and that's that.

Analysis: Even though this story is difficult to read due to mechanical and spelling errors, the writer attempts to convey the topic of the lemonade stand. There is also an attempt at logical order and an attempt at interesting words (*delicious*).

The Tasty Lemonade Stand   Score 1

The lemonade was tasty my lemonade is very yummy. The
people are nice. Soon a mean man laughted and said "ha ha ha."
They said "oh no!" It was Karl. They got $95.

Analysis: This story has a lot of unrelated things going on at once. One point was given for attempting interesting words (*tasty* and *yummy*). The story does not stick to the topic or have any logical order.

Writing Prompt

Intermediate Grades

Frogs in Love

It is Valentine's Day at the pond! Write a story about two frogs. Do the frogs have names? Where do they live? Do they fall in love? Do they live happily ever after?

Score 6

Frogs in Love

One day, a lonely frog named Amber was resting on a lilly pad in the creek. Just then, a handsome frog prince crossed her tracks. She stared, lovestruck.

"Where are you going?" she asked.

"To the pond dance, to see who I will marry," he replied.

"Oh, can I come?"

But he had already left, so she decided to follow him. "What do I have to lose?" she thought.

The pond was a beautiful, romantic sight. There were twinkling lights and soft music. Crickets chriped from the side lines. Amber watched the prince dancing in the moonlight with a humongous bull-frog that she knew wasn't his type.

"I wonder who my sweetheart will be?" the prince wondered, just at that moment. Suddenly he saw Amber on the muddy bank. He hopped over to her, took her smooth, slimy, green hand, and asked her to dance. It was a Valentine's Day she would remember for the rest of her life. Ribbbbitttt!

Analysis: This story receives a point in every category. It definitely sticks to the topic of two frogs meeting and falling in love on Valentine's Day. The story easily progresses from beginning to its relatively strong conclusion. *Romantic, twinkling, chirped,* and *humongous* give the piece its point for interesting words. The story flows easily because of the variety of sentence types. Descriptive phrases such as *beautiful, romantic sight . . . twinkling lights and soft music . . . muddy bank . . .* and *smooth, slimy, green hand . . .* give the piece its fifth point. Conversations between the frogs and the concluding "Ribbbbitttt" give the piece its 6th point for audience.

Score 5

Frogs in Love

What a day! It all started when Fred Frog wanted to give his girl-friend Fern the perfect valentine. Fred asked his friend Frank if he had any suggestions. Frank merrily answered, "Why don't you give her a boquet of flowers? If she has her own pad she'd probably like that."

Fred was to much in a hurry to say something in return. He was on his way to the pond to ask his cousin Fats if he had any advice. Fats croaked, "How about candy? I've never known a women who could refuse chocolate covered flies."

"Maybe," said Fred. Instead he hopped on to the next friend for advice.

"It doesn't matter what you give her, as long as you get it to her on the right day."

"Right day? What do you mean?"

"Valentine's Day was yesterday."

"OH . . . CROAK . . . NO!!!"

He leaped away as fast as he could, knowing that Fern was not going to be pleased. In fact, she was going to be HOPPING mad!

Analysis: This writer received 5 points. The narrative definitely sticks to the topic and has an order that is easy to follow. There were a few somewhat-challenging words (*suggestions, merrily, bouquet, probably, advice*). The direct quotations give the piece a variety of sentence patterns and a number of exclamatory comments *(What a day! . . .OH . . . CROAK . . . NO! . . . she was going to be HOPPING mad!)* are directed to the audience. The only thing lacking in this piece is descriptive sentences.

Score 4

Frogs in Love

There was only days left till valentines day in the creek. Finally, it was valentines day and two frogs jumped on the same lilypad. The girl thought the guy was very handsome so she gave him a glittery valentine. Feeling very romantic, he gave her a present of chocolate candy and croaked a melody. They exchanged hearts and promised to be true to one another. They grabbed each others slippery hand and croaked love songs until the moonlight shone on them.

Analysis: This is a typical Score 4 paper. The writer sticks to the topic, has logical order, and a few interesting words (*romantic, exchanged, promised, croaked, shone*). Use of varying sentence patterns (*Finally, it was . . . Feeling very romantic, he . . .*) and several compound sentences give it the final point.

Score 3

Frogs in Love

One day two lovesick frogs met one another at a pond. The boy frog ask the girl frog is she would be his valetine. She said yes so they jumped onto the lily pad. They went to the creek and he gave hersome flowers and said she was his sweetheart. In the moonlight he kissed her and said good night.

Analysis: This piece receives a Score 3 for sticking to the topic, having logical order, and varying sentence patterns. There is little attempt at interesting vocabulary (*pond, creek, moonlight*), and no attempt at descriptive sentences or audience.

Score 2

Frogs in Love

One day centuries ago it was Febuary 14 and by a pond there was a girl frog, and a handsome prince. They knew it wouldn't work being a prince so the frog thought a minute he jumped up and kissed her sweetheart. So they hopped on a lily pad and stayed there croaking and that made the valentines day.

Analysis: This piece basically sticks to the topic, but it is confusing because of the sentence structure. Logical order is attempted, but the story is very hard to follow. Vocabulary is basic for this grade level.

Score 1

Frogs in Love

The frogs favfit day is valentines day. Last year he wanted mary to be his valetine but she didn't.

Analysis: One point is given for the attempt to stick to the topic.

Once students have become familiar with a Score 6 anchor paper, it is time to share an actual state assessment rubric. Teachers will notice that on these holistic rubrics, the scoring addresses proficiencies in many areas at once. This type of writing rubric doesn't typically assign a point for each thing you do. However, it's the cross referencing, multiple-skill decisions that make the traditional rubric so hard to use. Using *The Simple 6™*, students and teachers simply ask whether or not each component of the rubric was **done well**. If yes, a point is given. If not, no point is given. There are times, however, when it's hard to tell if the point was given for interesting words or descriptive sentences. Sometimes it is also difficult to distinguish between sentence patterns and audience. In those cases a half point may be given in each area, making the final score more reliable. Half points should only be given between two closely-related components so the final score is always a whole number. Remember: The focus should be more on whether or not all students received a score of four or higher, rather than if a specific paper is a Score 4 or Score 5.

While this is not the traditional way to subjectively score a piece of writing with a complex rubric, it comes very close to or matches the score given by analyzing the piece through the traditional rubric scoring method. It would be great to think that all scorers would arrive at the same assessment score every time, but the subjectivity of writing makes that an unreasonable expectation. Writing scores on state assessments are appealed every year. And while we would like to think that the more complex the rubric, the more consistent the scoring, that is not always the case.

The focus at this point is not on comparing **The Simple 6™** *to* the individual state writing rubrics and arriving at the same score (even though it may very well happen). The point here is to ask students and yourselves, *"Do you now understand what is expected for a writing sample to be considered proficient? Do you know what qualities specifically contribute to a piece that passes? Can you now look at a piece of writing and tell whether it is exemplary or not, and why?"* By this time, the answer to these questions should be **YES** – and it doesn't matter if the people answering the questions are second graders or their teachers! Without a doubt, everyone should now **understand** what is expected.

Divide students into groups of three or four. Each group needs a writing sample, either on paper, computer, or overhead projector. Making sure the samples are double or triple spaced will make it easier for students to revise. It makes it easier if the samples are typed. Use a student writing sample from a previous year (making sure there is no student name on it), make up one yourself, or get a lower-scoring sample from the anchor papers provided by your state department of education.

Writing Samples that need to be revised

Primary: My Family by Zoe, Grade 2

I like my family. I Love my Mom and my Dad. I Love my

ginepig. I Like my family bacase thay are nise.

Intermediate: The Fifty Cent Wish by Allen, Grade 4

One day Brandon, Holly, skylar and I went to the grand fair

which only comes once a year. They saw a sign that said "Wish

Giver". They were the only people curious enough and brave

enough to go inside. When they got inside they found a man that

was tall and slender. His jet black hair was wetted down on his

head. He asked for 50 cents from each of us. He put our money

in his poket. He pulled out 4 cards with 2 spots on each card. He

gave one to Brandon, one to Holly, one to Skylar, and one to me.

He said, "Each card will grant one wish. All you have to do is walk

around in circles three times and then say your wish."

Middle School: My Favorite Vacation Spot by Kyle, Grade 6

I am going to tell you about my favorite place to camp. My

favorite place to camp is at Eby's Pines camp ground. The reason

why is because they have two under ground pools. One of them is

for lounging and the other has two slides that make you go realy

speedy and splash into the water. And back at the camp grounds

the cool sites have a creek behind them. You can also build an

open fire to cook on or just to admire. Theres a lot of bike trails

to ride. You can have a lot of fun there!

Give each student a mini rubric to attach to the piece being evaluated. Now that they have been exposed to scoring, let's take it one step further. It's not just enough to "do it well" to get a point. There must be evidence of mastery of the skill, and that means the scorer must see it more than once. As students (and teachers) score, put tally marks to the right of each component as evidence of mastery is seen. As a general rule, if a component has at least three tally marks, a point is given. Students should finish their scoring individually and then meet in small groups for discussion. They should identify areas of the paper that are weak and offer suggestions for improvement. When this task is completed, students are usually so excited that they want to do more than one.

Displaying the writing piece on the computer or overhead, discuss the scores and weaknesses as a class. This discussion might be led by the teacher or a student, depending on the age and ability of the students. Remember, we can simplify the process of scoring student writing, but it will never be easy. It's OK to disagree, as long as there is justification for the argument. Scoring should never be a guess.

As a second activity have students follow the same format with another writing sample, or give a different sample to each group. When all groups are finished, collect the papers for use on Friday.

Week 8: Peer Scoring and Revision   Friday/Day 2

Before they start any revisions, the group should attempt to score the piece as it is. This discussion will help to identify points of the rubric that may be the weakest in the piece. It will also help to put the piece into scoring perspective before students start looking for areas to improve. Attach a scoring rubric before students start revising. Here is a guide to help students stay on track:

Attack it!
Does the writing stick to the topic?
Is there a beginning, (three) middles, and an end?
Are the middles based on the questions in the prompt?

Simple 6™ it!
Can you improve the words?
Can sentence patterns be changed so it doesn't sound like a list?
Do you see several strategies being used to write descriptively?
     (precise verbs, proper nouns, adjectives, more details,
     literary techniques)
Is there an audience connection?

By this time students are confident about the 6 points. Have them work together to make corrections and improvements as they work through the rubric. When they are finished, have someone in the group read it aloud. This will help other group members listen for fluency and logical order. Depending on the age of the group members, this is a good time to consult a thesaurus to make sure all the generic words have been replaced. The group might also create a Word Bank.

When students are confident they have a Score 6, have a group member recopy or type the final draft. Publishing of the new piece can be accomplished in a number of different ways. Encourage groups to share by reading orally to the whole class and discussing the points of the rubric after the reading. An overall score might be assigned by discussion and general consensus of the whole group. Students might type the piece and exchange it with another group, getting their input on the final score. Another idea is to type the piece and place it on a bulletin board that has been divided into rubric score blocks. After a team evaluates the piece, they place it in the appropriate block, explaining why they decided to put it there.

Week 8: Scoring and Revision   Follow-up Activities

* Students rotate to four stations. Each station has a different anchor paper. Students have five minutes at each station, scoring the piece with the mini rubric and placing their rubric in the slotted box at each table. After 20 minutes discuss scores in a large group.

* Students play "**What's Missing?**" Rotating to four stations, they have 10 minutes to read, discuss, and decide why an anchor paper received a Score 5 instead of Score 6.

* Exchange papers with another class (without names). Score the papers and offer suggestions for improvement.

* Explain that all newspaper articles are read by an editor before they are published each day. Make up a 3-column front page filled with stories that need revision. Divide into groups. Let each group revise the story and republish the front page.

* Have everyone in the class anonymously contribute an old piece of writing. Put a copy of each student's piece in a large box. Let everyone in the class draw a story from the box to score and offer suggestions. (Variation: All students score and revise the same story individually. Then share).

* Type three stories on one sheet. Put the scoring rubric out to the side of each story. Have all students score individually. Compare and discuss.

Your ideas:

_____

_____

_____

_____

_____

_____

Lesson Plan: Scoring and Revision Day 1

Title   **Peer Scoring and Revision**   **Minutes: 60 minutes**
Source: *The Simple 6™: A Writing Rubric for Kids*

Behavioral Objectives: **Students will:**
- read and discuss anchor papers.
- be introduced to a holistic state scoring rubric.
- score papers using *The Simple 6™ method.*
- justify and defend their scores.
- offer suggestions for improving a piece.

Academic Standards: Writing Process: Evaluation and Revision

Materials Needed: anchor papers or other student writing, mini rubric

Introduction:
Who would like to lead the review?

Lesson:
Today we are going to score some actual writing assessments. Before we begin we will look at some that have already been scored. It's always a good idea to look at the best examples first, so we are going to look at a Score 6 paper, and then we will talk about why it received a Score 6. Continue the discussion until all students are clear about why the paper was exemplary.

Guided Practice:
You will each score an actual writing sample now. You will put your score on the mini rubric. For each component of the rubric that was done WELL you may give one point. When you are finished you will discuss the scores and reasons with your group members. The idea is not to try to convince the people in your group to change their scores to match yours. You will just be verbalizing your thoughts about the piece. Then we will compare the groups' scores and ideas. If there is time, students may engage in a second activity.

Conclusion:
How many of you feel more confident about scoring now? How many of you can see weaknesses in a piece of writing now? How has this helped your own writing?

Assessment:
Informal assessment-teacher observation.
  Did everyone participate?
  Were scores relatively close to one another?

Reflection:

Lesson Plan: Scoring and Revision Day 2

Title: **Peer Scoring and Revision**   **Minutes: 60 minutes**
Source: *The Simple 6™: A Writing Rubric for Kids*

Behavioral Objectives: **Students will:**
- score a piece of writing.
- defend their scoring decisions.
- identify weaknesses in writing prompts.
- make suggestions for revision.

Academic Standards: Writing Process / Evaluation and Revision

Materials Needed: anchor papers or other student writing, mini rubrics

Introduction:
Who would like to lead the review of *The Simple 6™* components today? Stick to the topic, have logical order, use interesting words, make different sentence patterns, write descriptive sentences, write for a specific audience.

Lesson:
Yesterday we learned to score a piece of writing. Today you each have a mini rubric, and you will score the piece that is on the overhead. It should take about five minutes for you to read it, score it, and jot down a few notes for revision.

Guided Practice:
In a small group you will discuss the scores. Did most of you agree, or were you within one point of one another? Talk about the weak areas of the piece. Contribute your suggestions for improvement. Rewrite the piece as a group. You may divide the group in half if that is easier. When you are finished have someone in your group retype the piece so a transparency can be made.

Conclusion:
What did you learn today about scoring? Did you come to the group with ideas for revision? How many feel that your group's revised piece is a Score 5 or Score 6?

Assessment:
Informal assessment-teacher observation.
Did everyone participate?
Can every student score a piece of writing and be within one point of everyone else?
Can students easily see where the weaknesses are?

Reflection:

Week 9: Creating and Sharing a Score 6   Day 1/Thursday

Never underestimate the importance of modeling exemplary writing. Now that students have all the necessary components for writing a great piece, it is still important to work with them as they perfect their writing techniques. Week 9 focuses on putting it all together, convincing students that they now have the ability to express themselves at the highest level. Your biggest task this week is to model, but this is also the perfect time to review the different types of writing.

Narrative writing tells a story

- Can be real or imaginary
- Has characters, setting, plot
- Includes vivid descriptions
- Follows beginning, middle, end pattern
- Ends with a conclusion or solution to a problem

Expository writing gives information

- Explains something
- Gives directions
- Tells about an event or memorable situation
- Requires thought and planning
- Follows the idea in a topic sentence
- Contains many supporting details

Persuasive writing attempts to change the opinion of the reader

- Supports opinion with facts and examples
- Requires logical, inferential thinking
- Focuses directly on the target audience
- Is heartfelt and personal
- Follows a topic sentence, supporting details or arguments, conclusion format

Descriptive writing paints a vivid picture of what is in the writer's mind

- Focuses on details
- Uses precise verbs and powerful adjectives
- Names things
- Illustrates events clearly
- Appeals to the reader's senses
- Uses other literary techniques

To emphasize growth, remind students of the dog we talked about on the first day of the nine week project. Using the same topic, students are ready for a Score 6 dress rehearsal. This session will be timed for 55 minutes, which is a reasonable amount of time for this task. Assessment times vary from 25 – 70 minutes throughout the U.S. Use the time that is appropriate for your situation.

Writing Prompt

Which One?

Your parents have finally given you permission to have a dog, and you are on your way to pick one out. The car stops, and . . .

Be sure to include:
- Where you are
- What you see...hear...smell
- Which dog you chose
- Why you chose that dog

Brainstorming (with [pink] Paper: 5 minutes)

Organizing (with **BME** paper: 10 minutes)

} **OR Prompt Attack (15 minutes)**

Writing the Rough Draft ([yellow] lined paper, every other line: 15 minutes)

TAKE A BREAK. ALLOW STUDENTS TO GET UP, GET DRINKS,

OR

VISIT WITH ONE ANOTHER FOR FIVE MINUTES.

Reading, Revising, and Editing (with red pens: 10 minutes)

Writing the Final Draft (white paper, formal heading, neat writing: 15 minutes)

Reviewing the Rubric as Questions   **Day 2/Friday**

Remember, when the rubric was originally written, it was designed as a set of guiding questions. This is a good time to go back and ask those questions, renewing understanding of each part of the rubric. Choose your weakest student to lead this discussion.

The Simple 6™ Questions

Did you **stick to the topic,** or did you run away with some other idea?

Have you presented your thoughts in a **logical order** that included an inviting beginning and a strong conclusion?

Have you overused generic vocabulary, or have you gone back to look for opportunities to use **interesting words?**

Did you use **different sentence patterns,** or does your story sound like a list?

Does each paragraph have a topic sentence and supporting detail **sentences that are descriptive?**

Did you write for an **audience?**

Give students some options at this point in time. As they attempt to write a piece that is a Score 6, they have the choice of walking through the whole process as a large group, having a prompt given to them, writing alone, or writing with a partner or in a small group.

GREAT IDEA!

If they choose working in a small group, divide students into groups of three or four. Each group needs a writing sample, either on paper, computer, or overhead projector. Making sure the samples are double or triple spaced will make it easier for students to revise. It is also easier to work with typed samples. Use a student writing sample from a previous year (making sure there is no student name on it), make up one yourself, or get a lower-scoring sample from the scoring booklet from your state department of education.

Before they start any revisions, the group should once again attempt to score the piece as it is. This discussion will help to identify points of the rubric that may be the weakest. It will also help to put the piece into scoring perspective before students start looking for areas to improve. Attach a scoring rubric before students start revising.

If students decide to work individually it's time for them to go back to their writing folder and choose a piece that they wrote very early in the process. It might even be the baseline writing sample they submitted on the first day of school. It can be from the formal writing folder, or it can be a piece of writing they have written at a writing center and have kept. It doesn't really matter, but every student should choose the particular piece he is interested in rewriting.

By this time students are pretty confident about the 6 points. Encourage them to work through the questions presented in *The Simple 6*™ as they revise and edit. This process and the completion of the final draft should be accomplished in about 30 minutes. Remember to remind students that even though they are trying to achieve a Score 6, the real goal is for every single student in the class to get at least a Score 4. If it happens today, on their first time out, don't forget to celebrate!

SAMPLES FROM DAY 2/FRIDAY ACTIVITY GRADE 4

Alyssa - rough draft

Editor Alyssa   **Date** 1-30-03

A Rainy Day

On Friday it was raining and school just

let out. When I got home I ~~play~~ *played* a game ∧ *called* *Yoshi Island*

A *I played thar game*
~~after~~ ~~the game~~ I ~~told~~ *asked* my mom if I could call

because such as sweet
she's a little girl
my friend and she said yes.∧ I ~~said to~~ *asked* my ~~told~~

asked

and
mom can she spend the night at my house she

Elise
arrived to
said yes. When my friend ~~got to~~ my house

at red lobster, I love
we eating there. got
we went out to eat ~~and~~ when we came home

until 3 in the morning
then we got
we stayed up and watch*ed* T.V. and ~~went to~~

some rest,
~~bed.~~ ~~then~~ When we woke up we had coco

puffs, then it was time for Elise to leave.

We got on are coats and drove away in my

huge van.

Score 6   final paper

A Rainy Day by Alyssa

On Friday it was rainy and school just let out. When I got home I played a game called Yoshi Island. After I played the game for a little bit I asked my mom if I could call my friend and she said yes she's such a sweet little girl. I asked my mom if she could spend the night at my house, and she said yes. When my friend Elise arrived at my house we went out to eat at Red Lobster, I love eating there. When we got home we stayed up and watched T.V. until three in the morning then we got some rest. When we woke up we had Coca Puffs, and then it was time for Elise to go home. We got on are coats and drove away in my huge van.

Skylar - rough draft

Editor <u>Skylar</u>   **Date** <u>1-30-03</u>

A Rainy ^school Day

On Friday it was raining and school just

let out. When I got home I ^wanted to play a game.

^A after the game I ~~told~~ ^asked my mom if I could call

my ^best friend ^Hannah and she said yes. I ~~said~~ ^O.K. to my

mom can ~~she~~ ^Hannah spend the night at ~~my~~ ^our house? she
^"you can, dear."

said yes. When ~~my friend~~ ^she ~~arit~~ ^arrived at got to my house

we went out to eat and when we ~~came home~~ ^got to my ^house
^at my favorite resturant "Between the Buns."

we stayed up and ~~watch~~ ^watched T.V. and went to

bed ^at 11:00 o'clock at night! Can you believe it!

The next morning Hannah had to
go home because she had a
Basketball game at 11:00 o'clock a.m.

Score <u>6</u>   final paper

A Rainy School Day by Skylar

On Friday it was raining, and school just let out. When I got home I wanted to play a game. So I did. After the game, I asked my mom if I could call my best friend Hannah, and she said, "Yes you can dear." I said to my mom, "Can Hannah spend the night at our house?" She said, "Yes dear." When she arrived at my house, we went out to eat at my favorite resturant Between the Buns, and when we got to my house we stayed up and watched T.V., and we went to bed at eleven o'clock at Night! Can you believe that? The next morning Hannah had to leave to go home because she had a Basketball game at eleven o'clock a.m. We had so much fun that night you wouldn't even believe it!

Week 9: Creating and Sharing a Score 6   Follow-up Activities

  * Put students in 6 groups. Place the rubric on the board. Each group focuses on only one component of the rubric. Read a sample paper. As each group decides whether that part of the rubric has been accomplished well, a student will come up and give the point (or not) for that component only.

* Have the teacher read a Score 6 paper each morning. After each reading, call on a student to come up to ask the questions:

Does this paragraph stick to the topic?   *Are sentence patterns varied?*
Does it have logical order?   *Are sentences descriptive?*
Are there interesting words?   *Was it written to an audience?*

* By this time the teacher should be confident and proficient at writing Score 6 papers. Using the overhead or computer screen, verbalize the entire thought process with the class as you write a paragraph. Do students agree that you have written a Score 6 paper? If not, why not?

Your ideas:

_____

_____

_____

_____

_____

Lesson Plan: Creating and Sharing a Score 6   Day 1

Title: **Creating a Score 6 Paragraph**   **Minutes: 60 minutes**
Source: *The Simple 6™: A Writing Rubric for Kids*

Behavioral Objectives: **Students will:**
• recite all the components of the rubric.
• practice scoring pieces of writing.
• write an exemplary piece.

Academic Standards: Writing Process / Organization and Focus, Evaluation and
                                                    Revision
                                                    Writing Applications / Narratives, Persuasive and Descriptive
                                                    Essays
                                                    Varied Word Choices
                                                    Audience –Style and Voice
                                                    Writing Conventions / Sentence Structure

Materials Needed: paper/pencil

Introduction:
Today you will have 55 minutes to create an outstanding piece of writing.

Lesson:
Consider this simple sentence:

The dog ran.

Think about all the strategies you have learned in the past eight weeks. Go through the checklist in your mind as you write and revise.

Guided Practice:
Using what you know about the writing process, I want you to focus on the prompt and create the highest scoring piece that you possibly can. I will be thrilled if you get a Score 6, but the goal is for every single one of you to get at least a Score 4.

Conclusion:
How many of you are confident that you did well? Did everyone finish on time?

Assessment:
Informal assessment-teacher observation.
   Did everyone participate?

Reflection:

Lesson Plan: Creating and Sharing a Score 6 Day 2

Title: **Creating a Score 6 Paragraph**   **Minutes: 60 minutes**
Source: *The Simple 6™: A Writing Rubric for Kids*

Behavioral Objectives: **Students will create a Score 6 paragraph.**

Academic Standards: Writing Process / Organization and Focus
Evaluation and Revision
Writing Applications / Narratives and Descriptive Essays
Varied Word Choices
Audience - Tone and Style
Writing Conventions /   Sentence Structure

Materials Needed: old writing sample

Introduction:
Today you will be given a choice of working alone or working with a group.

Lesson:
Everyone has a piece of writing that was considered to be finished at some point during the nine weeks. It has been written by you or by someone you don't know. You will have 30 minutes to read it, revise and edit it, and write the final copy. Remember to review the questions of *The Simple 6™* as you work through the process. Keep an eye on the time.

Guided Practice:
Make sure students are staying on task.

Conclusion
Students are now familiar enough with the expectations and the scoring to use this knowledge and these strategies to continue to improve their writing skills.

Assessment:
Informal assessment-teacher observation.
Is everyone in the Score 4 range? If not, continue to work with these students individually or in flexible skill groups, keeping track of growth on their data sheets.

Reflection:

Chapter 4

Writing Prompts

What should we ask students to write about?

Student Choice or Teacher-Generated Prompt?

Choosing the Best Prompt for Instructions:
The Skills
The Genre

Weekly Writing Prompt

What about NonFiction Expository Writing?

K-W-L Chart

Biography Research

Chapter 4   Writing Prompts

It takes practice and variation.
What should we ask students to write about?

Student Choice or Teacher-Generated Prompt?

The current trend in writing is for students to write about their own topics, with choice being the major motivator. Teachers are being encouraged to set aside at least 30 minutes of free writing time every day. Students are given plain paper, fun paper, chart paper, journals, binders, folders, and whatever they need to get their thoughts and ideas on paper. The more the better. Didn't feel like finishing a particular piece? This is not a problem. Students are encouraged to keep all these pieces of writing in various stages so they have a cache of samples to choose from on any given day.

Wednesday mini-lessons provide tips for writing, but the teacher's role in daily writing is primarily to provide assistance. During individual conferences students receive guidance through teacher questions and encouragement. Red pen days are over, and few pieces are actually collected and assessed. Many educators believe that the mere **experience** of writing will improve the skill, and that is certainly true – if students hadn't been writing at all.

For daily writing experiences, free writing is an excellent way for students to learn to express themselves. However, when student writing is formally assessed, choices are not given. All students write to a prompt in a very structured, timed environment. So while non-threatening, choice-driven writing activities are a necessary part of language arts instruction, **The Simple 6**™ promotes writing to a prompt during the nine weeks of instruction. This method provides consistency and clarity for students in a new learning environment and prepares them for the actual testing situation.

Choosing the Best Prompt for Instruction

THE SKILLS: The components of **The Simple 6**™ are introduced in the order of difficulty. Sticking to the topic is first, because if the writer veers from the topic the sample becomes invalid. Pieces of writing that progress logically and display some challenging vocabulary come next in the progression of student understanding. This is where the pass/no pass line is drawn. There is also a definite dividing line between the first three and the last three because it is when a student learns to vary sentence patterns and include descriptive details that the piece loses list-like quality. Writing for a specific audience is last because it is difficult to teach students how to get their writing to emanate a personal style. It is important to review the skills in order and to cumulatively review every week.

THE GENRE: The writing genre fall into four categories: narrative, expository, persuasive, and descriptive.

Narrative, or story writing, has all the elements of fiction – characters, setting, a central idea or problem, vivid descriptions of character interaction, and finally a conclusion or solution to the problem. Narrative writing can be long or short, funny or serious, realistic or extremely imaginative. Because of its range from simple to complex, it is appropriate for all age levels and is generally used with very young writers.

Expository writing explains or gives information. This type of writing requires thought and planning because the order of facts or events is important. Students might be giving directions, explaining the steps in a process, telling about a memorable event, or reporting information about something they are interested in. Expository writing lends itself more to the main idea – supporting detail – conclusion format, with the topic sentence leading the thought process. Expository writing can be something as simple as a telephone message or as complex as a report about electing government officials.

Persuasive writing gives students an opportunity to try to convince the audience to agree with their point of view. While persuasive writing is based on opinion, it must be supported with facts and examples. Logical thinking and inference are strong qualities of persuasive writing, and students must consider their audience when choosing the tone for the piece. The most important thing to remember about persuasive writing is that when students choose a topic that they really care about, they will write with more passion and try harder to find documentation to support their opinions. A few examples of persuasive writing include advertisements, book promotions, campaign speeches, or debates.

Descriptive writing paints a vivid picture of what is in the writer's mind and is interwoven throughout the other genre. In narrative writing, description plays an important role in clearly showing what is going on in the story – event by event. In expository writing description is used to relay information clearly. In persuasive writing powerful, descriptive language supports the writer's opinion and conveys passionate feelings about the topic.

The list of ideas for prompts is endless. As the prompt is chosen each week, consider the skill being focused, the genre of writing that is most appropriate, and the knowledge base of the students. The topic might reflect the students' personal knowledge, or it might be an extension of a current unit of study. Focusing on current events, holidays, TV shows, cartoon characters, current movies, or books can also help to extend the list. If students have to write without a background on the subject, no matter what it is, they will struggle. On the next page are some ideas for each point of the rubric.

<u>Stick to the Topic</u>   **Narrative, Expository, Persuasive**
My Favorite Pet
The Best Birthday Party Ever
My Best Friend
My Family

Literature/Reading:
Any current story character, theme, plot, or setting

Science:
Invertebrate animals-insects, worms
Vertebrate animals: mammals, reptiles, amphibians, birds, or fish
Weather
Plants
Pollution/Taking care of our environment

Social Studies:
Being a good citizen
Current news or events
Human interest stories
Catastrophes
Business/Economics-related news
Geographical locations
Cultural customs
Events in history
Famous people

<u>Logical Order</u>   **Narrative, Expository**

Retelling a well-known story
Retelling a story read by the teacher
The Time I went to . . .
My Trip to the . . .
The Fun Day
How to Make . . .
The Lost Homework
Planning a Vacation
The Great Surprise Party
The Missing Lunch Money
Cleaning my Room

<u>Interesting Words</u>   **Descriptive, Narrative, Expository, Persuasive**

Any topic that can relate to the following:
adjectives   being specific
choosing the best word   sensory perception

The First Snow
My Own Room
The New Baby
Halloween Night
The Lunchroom
Wonderful Word Wizard
Word Bank

Varied Sentence Patterns   Narrative, Expository, Persuasive, Descriptive

Have you ever wondered about how . . .
What if . . .
Have you ever been to the . . .
Direct quotations – stories with human characters
Animals that talk (Sam, the Talking Pig)
My Grandma
The Three Wishes
The Rainy Day
Mr. Wilson, my Next-door Neighbor

Descriptive Sentences   Descriptive, Narrative, Expository, Persuasive

Any topic with focus on the following:
    being specific
    sensory perception
    making your reader feel like he is there with you

Audience   Persuasive, Narrative

Matching style to reader
Letters
News Articles
Emotional pieces that convey seriousness, sadness, horror, humor
Fantasy-imagination
Familiarity-friend
Expert
The Camping Trip
A Recess to Remember
If I Could Fly

Prompt Format # 1: A Prompt with Questions

Understanding how prompts are organized is the key. The first paragraph usually sets up a scenario and offers some questions to be answered. The second paragraph always starts with directions for students. Those directions are usually followed by a review of the questions in the introductory paragraph. This time, however, they are in sentence format. A reminder box bullets those same questions and also gives reminders about planning and including as many details as possible. Here is an example of a prompt with questions.

An Exciting Day

Think of a time when you had an exciting day. Where were you? Who were you with? What happened to make your day so exciting?

Write a story about your exciting day. Be sure to tell where you were, who you were with and what happened to make your day so exciting. Include as many details as you can to make your story interesting.

Prompt Attack:

Introduction _____

Where were you?

(Exciting Day)

What happened?   Who were you with?

Conclusion _____

As students begin to write their rough drafts, have them check body paragraphs to make sure they like the order of events and have included ideas for details. They should have included an introduction that at least introduces the topic, and finished with a strong conclusion that leads into the end, tells exactly how everything turned out, and possibly adds their thoughts. For students who have not mastered paragraphing, Prompt Attack will keep everything in perfect order.

Prompt Format # 2: A Prompt without Questions

When the prompt has no questions students must write their own. Here is an example:

Prompt: The First Day of School

Write a story about your first day of school. It could be about your experiences this year or any other year. Include as many details as possible to make your writing interesting.

Teacher Introduction and Class Discussion:

Lead students in a discussion about doing something for the first time. The experience can be fun, exciting, or scary. What first-time experiences come to their minds? (riding a four-wheeler, auditioning for a play, riding a huge roller coaster, going to a piano lesson, going to bat in Little League, riding on a plane, giving a report in front of the class. . .) Choose one to do together.

Make a list of questions that come to their minds:

What was the experience?   Where were you?
How did you get there?   Who were you with?
What were you wearing?   Can you describe everything that happened?
What were you thinking and feeling? Would you do it again?

Now ask students to carry over these ideas into their story about The First Day of School, adding other questions if needed. They should choose three questions that will make up the body of their story. Place the questions on the Prompt Attack template.

Q1: _____

(First Day of School)

Q3:_____   Q2: _____

Conclusion:

As students answer the questions in complete sentences, they should ask themselves if the order of the answers feels right. If so, continue by writing key words or ideas under the answer to each question. If not, change the order of the paragraphs. Once planning is completed for the introduction and conclusion, students may start their rough drafts.

Prompt Format # 3: A Prompt Based on a Theme

Theme: Fairness

Think about a time when something happened to you that you thought was unfair. Write a story about what happened.

Again, because the prompt has no questions students must generate a list of their own.

What was not fair?   Where was I?

Who did the unfair thing to me?   Why do I think it wasn't fair?

How do I feel?   What can I do about it?

Choose the three questions that will make the best body paragraphs and start to complete Prompt Attack.

Q1: What was not fair?

_____

_____

Q3: What can I do about it?   **Q2: Why do I think it wasn't fair?**

_____   _____

_____   _____

Proofread!

No matter what type of prompt format is used, students should also be encouraged to proofread before turning in their work. Here is a list of questions students might ask themselves:

Did I capitalize the first word in each sentence?

Did I capitalize all proper nouns?

Did I end each sentence with the correct punctuation?

Do my nouns and verbs sound right together?

Did I spell words correctly? If I know it's wrong, did I ask for help?

Does my story make sense?

Weekly Writing Prompt

Title: _____

Teacher Introduction or Warm Up:

Student Warm-up/Brainstorming:

Student Directions:

Topic: _____

Questions:_____

_____

_____

_____

Editing Checklist:

Did you capitalize the first word in each sentence?

Did you capitalize all proper nouns?

Did you end each sentence with the correct punctuation?

Do your nouns and verbs sound right together?

Did you spell correctly?

Did you review each component of *The Simple 6™*?

What about Nonfiction Expository Writing?

Whether students are writing biographies, science reports, or developing social studies research projects, the foundation of all nonfiction writing is FACTS. Students must have facts and a general knowledge base before they can begin nonfiction writing, so it only makes sense that we first give students time to collect factual information.

Ideas for Class Discussion

1. Think of the big picture.

What is the main topic? Can sub-topics be identified? If you give students a very broad topic, there is more chance for them to find a sub-topic that interests them.

2. Consider possible sources.

Where can you find information about this topic? Make a list of sources. Start collecting your resources. The Internet is at your fingertips, but don't forget the importance of books, magazines, interviews with experts, newspaper articles, and other valuable sources.

3. READ.

Are you sure you still want to keep your original topic? As you read, you may find out that you want to alter your topic. There may be more information on a different aspect than what you had originally intended to write about. You may also find that the more you read, the more interested you are in another branch of the topic.

4. Collect factual information.

How are you going to remember all these new facts? You will need to write down the important information you learn. Use index cards or a spiral notebook for note taking. Don't forget to write your source at the top of the page. You may also want to make hard copies of information you get online.

5. Organize and store data.

Do you have a pocket folder? Where will you put your notes?

6. Design a framework.

How will you organize your writing? If you are writing more than one paragraph are you answering a specific question for each paragraph? Have you focused your writing on the information you found?

7. Review the rubric.

8. Write your rough draft.

Continue to think of the components of *The Simple 6*™ as you write your rough draft. It's easier to write nonfiction if you have an outline or question format in mind. Did you organize your information in advance?

9. Read, revise, consult with your teacher or peers. Then write the final copy.

Did your reader learn anything new?
Is your message clear?
Have you asked a few friends to read your work before you start the final copy?
Is it the best it can be?
Is it interesting and descriptive?
Is it filled with specific vocabulary that clearly states the information you are trying to convey to the reader?
Is your style appropriate for nonfiction writing?
Did you tie everything together at the end?

10. Present and share what you have learned.

Oral, Written, or Display

Nonfiction Fact Collecting: Question Format

1. What topic are you going to write about? _____

2. What do you want to know about this topic?

_____

(Make a **K-W-L** Chart on another piece of paper.)

3. Can you think of question words that might help you explore this topic?

   Where. . .

   When. . .

   How. . .

   What. . .

4. Where do you plan to look for your information?

_____

_____

_____

5. What web sites have you found for this topic?

_____

_____

_____

6. Do you have information from at least three sources?

_____

_____

_____

7. Based on the amount of information that is available, do you need to alter or adjust your original topic?

_____

8. Did you get enough information to answer many questions about this topic?

If not, which question(s) do you still need to answer? _____

_____

_____

9. Can you use these question words to help you organize the paragraphs in your report?

10. If your report is only one paragraph in length, did you get enough information about the topic to write at least three descriptive statements?

11. Can any of those statements be combined to make your sentence patterns more interesting?

12. How will you restate the topic sentence to make a strong conclusion?

Writing Checklist

Did you stick to the topic?

Does your information have logical order?

Did you use interesting words specific to your topic?

Did you combine ideas to write interesting sentences?

Did you write vivid descriptions based on the facts you learned?

Did you write for an appropriate audience?

Editing Checklist

Did you capitalize the first word in each sentence and all proper nouns?

Did you use the correct punctuation?

Are your sentences complete, and do your verbs agree with your subjects?

Did you look up words in a dictionary that you didn't know how to spell?

Nonfiction Fact Collection Sheet

I. Topic:

_____

Topic Sentence:

_____

_____

II. Detailed Facts (Let question words guide your research.)

_____

_____

_____

_____

_____

_____

_____

_____

_____

_____

III. Conclusion (Consider using a general statement, your personal opinion, or an intriguing question.)

_____

_____

_____

Name _____

Topic _____

K - W - L Chart

What I Know	What I Want to Know	What I Learned

Question Format for Biography Research

I. Background

    A. What is the person's full name?

    B. When and where was this person born?

    C. What was this person's childhood and family like?

    D. How was this person educated?

II. Adult Life

    A. Did this person marry and have a family?

    B. What kind of personality did this person have?

    C. What job or occupation did this person have before becoming famous?

    D. If this person is still living, what is he/she doing now?

III. Notoriety

    A. Why was (is) this person famous?

    B. Was (is) this person liked by the general public?

    C. Did this person have any nicknames, famous quotes, or speeches?

IV. Unusual Facts

    A. Was there anything unusual about this person?

    B. Are there any interesting or funny stories about this person?

V. Death

    A. When did this person die?

    B. How?

VI. Conclusion

    A. What feeling do you have about this person?

    B. What general statement describes this person's accomplishments?

Biography: Outline Format

I. Background Information

    A. Name/birth date/birthplace

    B. Childhood/Family

    C. Education

II. Adult Life

    A. Marriage/Family

    B. Personality (strengths/weaknesses)

    C. Other jobs or occupations

    D. Current status if still alive

III. Notoriety

    A. Contributions to society

    B. General public acceptance

    C. Famous quotes, speeches, nicknames

IV. Unusual or Little-known Information

    A. Unusual facts

    B. Stories or anecdotes

V. Death

    A. Date/place

    B. Cause of death

VI. Conclusion

    A. Your opinion

    B. Concluding statement or question

Chapter 5

Expanding Successes for Secondary Students

Same Ideas - Just a Little More Sophisticated

The Importance of Baseline Writing Samples

A Guide for Different Kinds of Writing

Modification for Students with Varying Abilities

Working within a Non-threatening Format

Reviewing the Basic Framework of a Paragraph

Writing Across the Curriculum

A Writing Rubric for Secondary Students

Scoring

Anchor Papers

© 2009 Pieces of Learning
The Simple 6™ Revised Edition

Chapter 5   Expanding Successes for Secondary Students

Same Ideas — Just a Little More Sophisticated

The Simple 6™ for Secondary Students very closely follows the format of *The Simple 6™ for Kids.* The only difference is the level of sophistication in the wording of the rubric and how you will use it with writers of various levels.

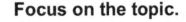

Focus on the topic.

Check for logical order.

Use challenging vocabulary.

Include varied sentence patterns.

Include exceptional supporting details.

Display a strong sense of audience or style.

The Importance of Baseline Writing Samples

Take a baseline sample from every student on the first day of class – no matter what subject you teach. The only thing you have to remember is whether or not they have a **knowledge base.** Students can write about a specific topic you know they have already studied such as safety, getting along, being responsible, why they are taking the class, what they hope to learn this year, peer pressure, how this class will help them later in life, their favorite job, etc. You might also consider something simple like: an apple, a paperclip, their favorite TV commercial, a certain type of car. You could also use the old standbys: family, best friend, goals, pets, If I had $1,000, etc. If the topic is appropriate for their age and interests, anything will work. Just do it!

Students at the secondary level will be coming to you from many levels of writing expertise. The importance of baseline writing samples, however, has nothing to do with the grade you are teaching. A piece of writing gives invaluable information to you about the students' attitude, overall language arts abilities, listening skills, attention to detail and neatness, and their ability to follow a short assignment through to completion.

In addition to giving you information about individual students, use the writing sample as a jump-start indicator of the types of skills you will need to teach as Wednesday mini-lessons. Even in classes that are tracked for above-average students, there is always room for improvement. In the unlikelihood that you have several Score 6's on the first day, use them as examples and go from there. You may have such outstanding writers that your goal will be to have every student publish something in a professional journal.

The most valuable use for the first-day writing sample is for the students to realize their own growth throughout the semester. You may give the assignment on the first day of school, collect it, and not mention it to students for several weeks. By the time they have become familiar with three to four parts of *The Simple 6*™, they are amazed at the number of obvious components they "left out" of their original piece. Many will also want to use that piece as a springboard for revision and bring it to completion later in the year.

A Guide for Different Kinds of Writing

As students get older, **narrative writing** seems to take a back seat to other, more sophisticated types of writing. Narrative writing, however, is a natural and appropriate complement to the study and analysis of literature. All the elements of a story fall into place as students focus on sticking to the topic, logical order, and exceptional supporting details. Also, just because students are older doesn't mean that imaginative writing should be eliminated from their curriculum.

Students at the secondary level are able to focus more on detail and precise language. They should have many opportunities for **descriptive writing** that reflect their reading, their attitudes, and their surroundings. Descriptive writing should be filled with exceptional language and sentences that create powerful illusions.

Expository writing, which lends itself to more straight-forward presentation of facts, can still be assessed with *The Simple 6*™. While students are rarely given an expository writing prompt on a standardized assessment, mastering this kind of writing is essential. Whether students are writing to explain or to report information, the rubric still offers a concrete guide to organization and clarity.

Persuasive writing gives adolescents an opportunity to voice their opinions – based on facts, of course! In this genre, style, voice and literary devices are used to speak directly to an audience. Students with more sophisticated critical thinking and inference skills can still rely on *The Simple 6*™ to keep their arguments supportive, organized, and focused on the topic.

© 2009 Pieces of Learning
The Simple 6™ Revised Edition

Modification for Students with Varying Abilities

The only difference between *The Simple 6™ for Kids™* and *The Simple 6™ for Secondary Students* is the level of sophistication by which the components are presented. 6th grade students with no prior experience in working with this rubric will benefit from first using *The Simple 6™ for Kids*. Older students who are considered at-risk or students with special academic needs may also find the elementary rubric easier to understand. Choose the rubric that is appropriate for the level of your students. You will get positive results with either one. It all depends on the ability and maturational levels at which your students are working.

For students with learning disabilities, **The Simple 6™** is an easy, straightforward guide to organization. Each component is easy to remember and use, especially if students have been given a chart-like copy of the rubric to keep in their writing notebooks. If students go to a resource room for additional help, a wall chart of **The Simple 6™** is a very effective tool for reinforcement.

If students have a great deal of difficulty following a story line, focus on one point of the rubric at a time. Most students can stick to the topic and follow a logical order in a relatively short period of time.

Based on the students' strengths and weaknesses, decide which component will be the easiest to add. Usually, with assistance, students can find three words that they can improve. Word Banks may need to be a part of the planning process, and students may have to be reminded that every piece of writing needs three wonderful words in it.

If learning-disabled students can accomplish that much, it is relatively easy to introduce the concept of varying sentence patterns. Something as simple as teaching the students to begin and/or end each piece with a question might get a point for audience as well as varying sentence patterns.

Don't be afraid to experiment with various components to see which ones your students prefer. Then really work on those skills. Remember, your special needs students are trying to get into the passing zone. Start with the basics, and add enough to get them into the Score 4 range – in their own way. Once they've mastered four you can consider adding a fifth. I don't recommend trying to master all six. It is just too much and too confusing. Focus on four elements, based on your students' strengths in writing.

Students with exceptional abilities will also benefit from **The Simple 6™**. Gifted/ talented students are not necessarily gifted writers. Some gifted students are so fact oriented that it is difficult for them to be creative and descriptive. Others have so much to say that they ramble on and on, straying from the topic because they have become interested in another facet of the subject. Gifted and talented writers, however, easily master the rubric because they can analytically break it down into intricate parts of a somewhat complicated puzzle.

The Simple 6™ is the secret to attaining the elusive Score 6. Whether you are 8 or 18, the rubric leads the way to understanding how writing will be assessed. The most important part of the process is consistency. If you commit to this method of teaching for nine weeks, your students will improve their scores. Why? Because you have helped them to understand the assessment process, you have taught them the skills they need to succeed, and you have given them opportunities to write, discuss, revise, and publish.

Working within a Non-threatening Format

There is nothing wrong with starting with a five-sentence paragraph, even with high school students. Length has little to do with writing ability. Secondary students who write page after page, rambling without direction, are no better off than the second grader who has little experience and a limited vocabulary. The basic fundamentals are the same. The topics have to be adjusted to fit the developmental level and interests of your students, however, if you want them to approach writing with interest and enthusiasm.

Reviewing the Basic Framework of a Paragraph

Reviewing the importance of the topic sentence, supporting details, and conclusion is always a good place to start. This framework should already be familiar to most students. For those hearing it for the first time, its concrete structure will be a stable place to begin. Give students two small pieces of paper. Ask them to write a topic on each one that they feel would be interesting and appropriate for the class. Collect all the papers. Draw out one topic and proceed to write a story together with the class – either on the board, on the overhead, or on the computer screen.

During this activity, you might come up with the topic sentence as a whole group. Then let students work in small groups for five minutes to come up with supporting detail sentences. Come back together as a large group, deciding which detail sentences to use. Have someone read the paragraph to get the flow, and then compose a conclusion as a class. Your discussion and guidance along the way will give students a non-threatening setting in which they become comfortable with writing. Then proceed, for the next nine weeks, to introduce or review the components of *The Simple 6™: A Writing Rubric for Secondary Students.* Follow the plans for the Writing Rubric for Kids, and adjust the level of instruction as needed.

Writing Across the Curriculum

Teachers in the content areas are also responsible for offering students regular writing opportunities. Focusing on an organized, content-based paragraph rather than a formal essay is meaningful and less time consuming. Ideas for writing can easily be integrated into unit lesson plans. Writing a paragraph that reviews the current content, answering test questions in essay format, and explaining how to solve a math problem are just a few examples of how writing activities can easily be integrated in non-English classes. *The Simple 6™* rubric can easily be used to assess paragraphs.

If The Simple 6™ were a complex holistic rubric for secondary students, it might look like this:

The Simple 6™: A Writing Rubric for Students					
	1 Poor	**3 Minimal**	**5 Competent**	**6 Exemplary**	**Total**
Focuses on the Topic	Attempts to focus on topic	Focuses on the topic	Focuses on the topic	Completely focuses on the topic	
Logical Order	Lacks order	Has logical order	Has an inviting beginning, descriptive body, and strong conclusion	Has fluent transitions, order that enhances meaning, an inviting introduction, and a powerful conclusion	
Challenging Vocabulary	Lacks challenging vocabulary	Attempts challenging vocabulary	Uses some challenging vocabulary	Uses concise, challenging vocabulary	
Sentence Patterns	Lacks varied sentence patterns	Sentences have list-like quality	Varies sentence patterns	Varies sentence patterns to enhance fluency	
Supporting Details	Lacks details	Lacks in-depth details	Has fully developed supporting details	Has fully developed, exceptional supporting details	
Audience	No audience connection	No audience connection	Tone and style are appropriate	Tone and voice make audience connection	
				Total	

Let these questions guide you:

1. Did you **focus on the topic**, or did you go off on some other tangent?

2. Have you presented your thoughts in a **logical order** with an inviting introduction, a strong conclusion, and smooth transitions?

3. Have you used **challenging vocabulary** to make descriptions rich and explanations detailed and precise?

4. Have you created **varied sentence patterns** and writers' techniques such as imagery, dialogue, humor, suspense, etc.?

5. Do you have **exceptional supporting details** that address all the specific points of the prompt?

6. Did you write for an **audience**? *(Did you write with an original, lively, authoritative tone; or did you use any other unique perspective that made a direct connection with the audience?)*

© 2009 Pieces of Learning
The Simple 6™ Revised Edition

A Writing Rubric for Secondary Students

Focus on the topic.
Check for logical order.
Use challenging vocabulary.
Include varied sentence patterns.
Include exceptional supporting details.
Display a strong sense of audience or style.

Ask these questions: yes = 1 point   no = 0 points

_____ Did you **focus on the topic,** or did you go off on some other tangent?

_____ Have you presented your thoughts in a **logical order** with an inviting introduction, a strong conclusion, and smooth transitions?

_____ Have you used **challenging vocabulary** to make descriptions rich and explanations detailed and precise?

_____ Have you used **varied sentence patterns an**d writers' techniques such as imagery, dialogue, humor, suspense, etc?

_____ Do you have **exceptional supporting details** that address all the specific points of the prompt?

_____ Did you write for a specific **audience?**

(Did you write with an original, lively, authoritative tone; or did you use any other unique perspective that was appropriate for the prompt?)

_____ **TOTAL POINTS** (How many did you answer yes?)

© Kay Davidson

Quick Reference Chart for Secondary Students

Focus on the Topic

- Focus on the topic and don't run away with other ideas.

- Follow the prompt instructions.

Logical Order

- BME (beginning, middle, end)

- Focus on the inviting introduction and the strong conclusion.

- Use the prompt to guide structure.

Challenging Vocabulary

- Include a minimum of three challenging vocabulary attempts.

- Eliminate generic words such as went, said, big, little, good, etc.

- Use new words correctly.

Varied Sentence Patterns

- Include questions, exclamations. and items in a series.

- Focus on complex sentences.

- Use dialogue, if appropriate.

- Use sentence patterns to make writing fluent.

Exceptional Supporting Details

- Use precise verbs.

- Include proper nouns.

- Insert adjectives - not too many.

- Use a variety of literary techniques.

Audience/Voice

- Write in a tone that is appropriate for the prompt.

- Make a direct connection to the audience.

- Let your personality shine!

© Kay Davidson, rev. 2007

Score 6 Expectations at the Secondary Level

It is important to keep in mind that a Score 6 is exemplary and not often given. This is not to say that a Score 6 should not be the goal, especially for advanced-track or gifted and talented students. The elusive Score 6 is not as elusive as it appears. This is what a Score 6 looks like:

The writer addresses ideas and content by staying **completely focused on the topic.** He addresses all the specific points of the prompt, while following a unified theme or main idea. His **supporting details are based on in-depth information** and are fully developed. He explores more than one aspect of the topic.

Organization is apparent. There is an **inviting introduction, a descriptive body, and a strong conclusion.** Transitions are fluent, and the writing progresses in an order that enhances the meaning.

Style is evident by the writer's use of **concise, challenging vocabulary.** Descriptions are vivid, explanations are detailed, and meaning is clear. The use of **varied sentence patterns** and complex sentences make the writing fluent. Imagery, dialogue, or literary genres show the writer's ability to demonstrate exceptional technique in communicating with an **audience.**

Scoring Directions

6 A Score 6 paper is consistently excellent from beginning to end, and therefore is rare.

   * focuses on the topic   * uses exceptional supporting details
   * displays logical order   * varies sentence patterns
   * uses challenging vocabulary * writes for an audience

5 The difference between a Score 6 and a Score 5 is often the lack of consistency, in-depth development, sophisticated sentence structuring, and/or challenging vocabulary.

   * focuses on the topic   * varies sentence patterns
   * displays logical order   * includes supporting details
   * uses challenging vocabulary or writes for an audience

4 A Score 4 paper represents a solid "passing" performance. One factor that differentiates a Score 4 from a higher score is the lack of *exceptional* supporting details. Vocabulary may not be as developed as on a Score 5.

   * focuses on the topic   * includes supporting details or challenging
                                          vocabulary

   * displays logical order   * varies sentence patterns

3 A Score 3 paper is associated with the word minimal. A Score 3 has a definite list-like quality.

   * focuses on the topic   * includes some details but they are not
                                          fully developed

   * displays logical order

2 A Score 2 communicates some ideas. The content is never really developed due to lack of language skills.

   * attempts to focus on the topic   * attempts to display logical order

1 The student conveys some meaning. Problems with sentence structure may limit the writer's ability to communicate ideas.

    * attempts to focus on the topic

© 2009 Pieces of Learning
The Simple 6™ Revised Edition

The Simple 6™

0 / 1

_____ Focus on the Topic
_____ Logical Order
_____ Challenging Vocabulary
_____ Varied Sentence Patterns
_____ Exceptional Supporting Details
_____ Audience

_____ TOTAL POINTS

Kay Davidson, Revised 2002

The Simple 6™

0 / 1

_____ Focus on the Topic
_____ Logical Order
_____ Challenging Vocabulary
_____ Varied Sentence Patterns
_____ Exceptional Supporting Details
_____ Audience

_____ TOTAL POINTS

Kay Davidson, Revised 2002

The Simple 6™

0 / 1

_____ Focus on the Topic
_____ Logical Order
_____ Challenging Vocabulary
_____ Varied Sentence Patterns
_____ Exceptional Supporting Details
_____ Audience

_____ TOTAL POINTS

Kay Davidson, Revised 2002

The Simple 6™

0 / 1

_____ Focus on the Topic
_____ Logical Order
_____ Challenging Vocabulary
_____ Varied Sentence Patterns
_____ Exceptional Supporting Details
_____ Audience

_____ TOTAL POINTS

Kay Davidson, Revised 2002

Anchor Papers

The following anchor papers are student-generated pieces of writing that have been scored using *The Simple 6™: A Writing Rubric for Secondary Students.* These samples are provided to give teachers an idea of the standard set at each level of the rubric. Attaching mini-rubrics to each piece makes it easy for teachers as well as students to document progress. They can also be used for peer assessment. Note: These examples are much shorter than formal, secondary essays.

Middle School

Winning the Lottery
- You have just won the lottery.
- What will you do with all that money?
- How do you feel?
- Will this change your life?

Score 6

If I won the lottery it would be for an enormous amount (like two trillion dollars), because I wouldn't buy a ticket otherwise. The first thing I would do is build a new cottage-type mansion in the country, where there was lots of space. Then I would spice up the house with new furniture and outstanding electronic devices. Next I will install an underground swimming pool with a nice big jacoosie. Since I'm such a sports guy though, I would have to install a football field, basketball court, track, and a racing strip for all my cars.

Aaaahhhh, the cars! There would have to be five impressive vehicles, with the first one being a Viper. I would install some NOS and give it a classy paint job. The second car would have be a Ferarri. It would have to be gold. After that I would get a lowridder. I would put some highdrolics in the back, spinning rims on all four wheels, and a huge stereo with speakers all around. The next car I would want is a Mark four Supra, with a twin turbo V-6 engine, and give it the works also. The last car I would want is a limo with soundproof glass and leather seats. That would be for important events only. I wonder how much it would cost to hire a driver?

> Then I would invite my friends over for an extravigant party and send a huge check to charity. I would never just hog all the money for myself. The last and final thing I would *do* is pay all the taxes, insurance, and rent on all the stuff I bought. Now that's what I call fun and excitement.

Analysis: This piece receives a Score 6. It definitely focuses on the topic and progresses logically with original ideas and exceptional supporting details. Challenging vocabulary includes *impressive, lowrider, hyighdraulics,* and *extravigant* – which is not the greatest for this grade level, but was appropriate for the piece. Various sentence structure is evident, as well as making a connection with the audience (*Aaaaahhhh, the cars! . . . I wonder how much it would cost to hire a driver? . . . Now that's what I call . . .*)

Score 5

As I watched the evening news, it was time for the powerball. The amount was HUGE this week ($60,850,000), so I convinced my parents to buy me a ticket. I paid for it with my allowance.

It was the moment of truth! I looked down at the tattered ticket that had been in my pocket all day. "It is now time to announce the powerball. The numbers are 421893562," said the newscaster.

"Oh my gosh! Oh my gosh! WE WON!" I shouted. Everyone was screaming and jumping for joy. My heart was pounding, yet somewhere in my brain I couldn't believe it was really happening.

The next moring we traveled to the news station to claim our check. I couldn't tell them that I had won because I wasn't old enough, but I knew what I wanted to do with the money. (Well, some of anyway. What does anyone do with that much money?) I would give most of it to my parents, give some of it to help the war, and keep the rest of it for my future in college.

Well, that was eight years ago, and I'm proud to say I did everything that I wanted to with my lottery winnings. I've graduated from Harvard, I have a career in acting and dancing. I write poems in my leisure time, and I've just published my first book. Just think. Would I have been able to accomplish all that without winning the lottery?

Analysis: The piece receives 5 points although it is not a strong 5. It definitely focuses on the topic and has logical order. The point for exceptional vocabulary is weak (*convinced, tattered, announce, newscaster, accomplish*). There are various types of sentence structure, and sentences are somewhat descriptive. This is probably a case where I would give half a point for vocabulary and half a point for descriptive sentences. The fifth point would be for audience (*Well, that was eight years ago, and I'm proud to say . . Would I have been able to accomplish?*)

Score 4

If I won the lottery, I would do many extraordinary things. I would buy an enormous mansion with an in-ground pool and a cedar sauna. It would be tan brick, and there would be lots of decorative landscaping in the yard. After that, I would give money to homeless shelters and charities.

After buying the mansion and giving money to charities, I would pay off the car payments on my Honda Civic and then I'd pay my taxes. (I've never had to worry about that before.) I would do the same for my family too. Then I would buy a huge play-ground with swings, tubes, and plastic balls. It would be open to my family and the children in my neighborhood.

After all of that, I would keep a small protion of my first installment. Finally, I would keep going to school so my life would be somewhat normal. I'd just keep going to school, and I'd be looking forward to those monthly checks!

Analysis: This piece receives four points for focusing on the topic, logical order, challenging vocabulary (*extraordinary, enormous, cedar, decorative,* and *installment*), and varied sentence patterns. No point was given for exceptional supporting details or audience.

Score 3

If I won the lottery I would do three main things with that money. These things are, I would put some in the bank, help people in need, and go on a shopping spree.

The first thing I would do with the money is I would put money in the bank. I would put money in the bank so when I get to college I can buy a car, and so I will have money for my books, and everything.

The second thing I would do with my money is I would help people in need. I would make duffel bags with toothbrushes, clothes, and games in them for people or homeles kids in our community.

The third thing I would do with my money, is I would take whatever is left over, and take my five best friends shopping. If I won the lottery I would be very happy knowing that I helped someone besides myself.

Analysis: This piece receives 3 points for focusing on the topic, logical order, and varied sentence patterns, although that is somewhat weak. There was no attempt to use challenging vocabulary, to write exceptional supporting details, or to write for an audience. The piece seems to be made of sentences that followed a specific outline and would not be considered passing.

Score 2

If I won the lottery I would spend it all of the money on play Station 2 games, and a huge movie screen.

If I recieved all of that then I would envite all of my friends and play games all day long.

And that is what I would do if I won the lottery.

Analysis: The piece receives two points for focusing on the topic and having logical order. Ideas and vocabulary are sparse. No attempt was made to connect with the audience.

Score 1

If I won the lottery I would go to Las Vegas wright away. And try and bye a hotel. And even have more money. Then my family could come down and go swimming. And one more thing is I would pay the tax person so much moeny.

Analysis: This piece would receive one point for attempting to focus on the topic, even though sentences and ideas are fragmented.

High School

Reflecting on Nature

- Take a moment to have a "Thoreau" experience.
- Go outside. Appeal to your senses.
- What feelings are inspired by nature?
- Reflect on your observations.

Score 6

Gazing from my window, everything appears peaceful and quiet. I am beckoned outside where the leaves lightly nip my ankles in the breeze. Birds chirp quietly as the sun is drawn to the horizon. The colorful hues of the sky, clinging to their vibrancy, are soft and slow to change. The dead leaves in the trees dance slowly, alone. The mere simplicity of it all mesmerizes me. As the stars slowly pierce the night sky I wonder, will there ever be another time just like this?

Analysis: This descriptive paragraph receives 6 points. It focuses on the topic, has logical order, challenging vocabulary, and varies sentence patterns. The descriptive details are exceptional, and the writer connects with the audience in the last sentence.

Score 5

The ancient oak tree's bony fingers reach out toward the clouds. The lower branches, though, slump over like an old woman. Most the leaves have fallen, but a few still pointlessly remain. The once beautiful, sienna bark is now cracked and peeling. The roots are exposed, quietly requesting shelter from the elements. Somewhere near the top of the tree, a pair of bluebirds chirp and then fly away. I wonder if this is what it is like to be old.

Analysis: This piece gets 5 points for focusing on the topic, having logical order, descriptive sentences but not necessarily challenging vocabulary, and varied sentence patterns. The writer connects with the audience at the end (*I wonder…*). If this piece had been longer it had potential to become a Score 6.

Score 4

Have you ever wondered what squirrels do on a lazy spring afternoon? Squirrels will run around, chase each other up and down trees, and spiral around and around the trees. They tease each other by chattering their teeth and flipping their tails. Then one will suddenly spring away towards the other and chase will start all over again. As I was watching them chase each other, they stopped towards the top of the two trees that are next to each other. I yelled "HEY!" The next thing I knew, they both fell out of the tree. One squirrel got up and ray away, but the other squirrel laid there. I thought he was dead, but after 15 to 30 seconds, he got up and ran away. This was the first time that I ever saw squirrels fall out of a tree!

Analysis: While this piece is marginal for high school, I would give 4 points for focusing on the topic, having logical order (even though the change in verb tense detracts from the flow), varied sentence patterns, and audience. Vocabulary is weak and supporting detail sentences are not very descriptive.

Score 3

As I look into the sky, I see the moon. Its luminous glow is quite brilliant. The moon looks so small in something so large-the sky. I know white is supposed to make something look big. I also know that black is supposed to make something look smaller. In this case however, it is just the opposite. The white moon and the black sky are the opposite of what is fact. The moon, smaller and the sky is larger.

Analysis: This piece receives only 3 points. The writer focuses on the topic, attempts logical order (although the conclusion is weak), and varies the sentence patterns. Descriptive sentences are attempted but low level. No point is given for audience.

Score 2

It was a Monday afternoon and it was so gorgeous outside. The sun was shining brightly and it was about 70 degrees. Spring was in the air, I noticed squirrels chasing and frolicking after each other. I also saw crocuses and daffodils poking their heads through the soil and taking a deep breath.

Analysis: This piece receives two points for focusing on the topic and exceptional supporting details. There is no logical order, which makes the piece seem incomplete. No attempt was made to use challenging vocabulary, vary sentence patterns, or to connect with the audience.

Score 1

Dogs running, kids playing, birds flying these are the images of nature. Nature relates to everything, especially humans. Nature is romantic just like humans. All of mankind has a little romanticism in them.

Analysis: This piece receives one point for attempting to focus on the topic. Ideas are fragmented and hard to follow.

Recommendation:

The Simple 6 ™ for Secondary Writers outlines the program for secondary students and provides teachers with cross-curriculum lesson plans, prompts, anchor papers, and revision strategies. Available from Pieces of Learning. Marion IL. www.piecesoflearning.com

Chapter 6

Language in Use:
The Four Point Rubric

What are Conventions?

Academic Standards for Conventions

You're the Teacher: Editing for Kids

Chapter 6   Language In Use: The Four Point Rubric

What are Conventions?
Mastery of mechanics is important, but it's a separate skill.

Language in use is also referred to as mechanics, conventions, grammar, or word usage. On most standardized assessments, this is a separate score. Conventions are usually graded on a four-point scale, with four skills being evaluated. The same rubric is used at multiple grade levels, and the expectations vary as the levels increase. While the academic standards provide a necessary guide for instruction, it is important to note that not all skills reflected in the standards are evaluated on the standardized assessment.

It is also important to note that national standards for language arts at specific grade levels are not available. However, individual states have written their own academic standards based on the guidelines of the National Council of Teachers of English. Some state assessments evaluate English mechanics or conventions as part of the content writing rubric. Other states have a separate rubric for conventions, which they also refer to as language in use or mechanics.

Again, proficiency is measured using a holistic rubric, but students can trade point for point or use questions as their guide. The four areas to focus on are capitalization, punctuation, complete sentences that have subject/verb agreement, and spelling. Consider the following questions:

Capitalization
Did you capitalize all proper nouns?
Did you capitalize the first word in each sentence?
Did you capitalize correctly in all parts of a letter?

Punctuation
Did you use the proper punctuation at the end of each sentence?
Did you use commas and quotation marks correctly?
Did you remember to use apostrophes in contractions and to show possession?
Did you punctuate correctly in a letter?

Complete Sentences with Subject/ Verb Agreement
Do all sentences have a subject and predicate?
Do your subject and verb agree with one another?
What about past, present, and future tense?

Spelling
Did you spell words correctly that are appropriate for your grade level?
Did you remember to use the correct homonym?
If you used outstanding words that you didn't know how to spell, were you careful to sound them out phonetically?
Did you proofread your final draft before turning it in?

Remember: All applications of language in use don't have to be perfect, but errors must be minimal to get full credit.

Practice Makes Perfect

You're the Teacher: Editing for Kids

Can you spare 15-20 minutes a week to guarantee your students will improve their editing skills? The best way to write error-free is to practice finding errors on papers that are already completed. Having fun in the process is definitely appealing to students, so every week a time is set aside for *You're the Teacher.* It takes about 15 minutes and is separate from instructional writing time.

Each Friday students take out their red pens and check a series of sentences that are filled with errors. These errors are based on the language arts standards for that particular grade level and follow recent Wednesday mini-lessons. The errors fall into three categories: capitalization, punctuation, spelling. Students must look for errors in all three categories at once.

By giving students 6 to eight sentences every Friday, telling them how many errors there are, and giving them hints about particular skills that might be focused on, the editing skills steadily improve. *You're the Teacher* is not designed for students to get 100% each week. It is designed to be a challenge, and students strive to be one of the few who find all the errors. The novelty of getting to "grade the paper" is the motivator. If there is a scheduling conflict that eliminates *You're the Teacher* on any given Friday, students voice their objections. There is something addictive about trying to find those mistakes every week. Students challenge one another and themselves to be the best editor in the class. This is the single most successful strategy I have ever used to improve student proofreading and editing skills, and I've used it for 30 years at every grade level.

The key to success in *You're the Teacher* is that once students are used to looking for three types of errors in each sentence, finding only one error per sentence on the standardized assessment is a snap. They slowly become much more adept at finding those mechanical and grammatical errors as they revise, and many start writing correctly on their rough drafts. For those students who still struggle with seeing the errors on their own papers, peer editing in a small group keeps their progress moving. Individual student-teacher conferencing is also helpful.

What about those students who just don't get it?

For those students who need extra help it's always best to simplify. The key is to teach students to focus. Two strategies I use for focusing are to concentrate on one skill at a time, and to concentrate on one sentence at a time.

In concentrating on one skill at a time, first talk to the student about that particular skill. For example, capitalization. Ask the student to tell you all the times you might use a capital letter. On a separate sheet of paper or index card, write the reasons as the student tells them. List the heading neatly on the top of the card, and talk the student through a few sentences where he is looking for capitalization only. As a follow up, and depending on the academic level of the student, you may have him find ONLY capitalization errors (and put a new, special number at the bottom of the paper). When 100% accuracy is achieved, move on to punctuation.

Concentrating on one sentence at a time is the way most students do **You're the Teacher.** Encourage everyone to use a ruler in the beginning. This stops those students who rush to capitalize every word on the left side of the paper (including those words that are the continuation of a long sentence). Students should evaluate the sentence in the following order: capitalization, punctuation, and spelling. When they are satisfied that they have found all the errors, they move on to the next sentence and do the same thing.

A note about spelling: Young students struggle and use up a lot of time looking up words in a dictionary. I have found it much more time-efficient and appropriate to use write-in spelling dictionaries. The Quick Word: Handbook for Everyday Writers by Curriculum Associates, Inc. is a good choice. These consumable booklets contain words most often used at a particular grade level with blanks on each page for students (or the teacher) to write in student-requested words. This dictionary is personal and level-appropriate for each student. Because the students use these dictionaries during regular writing activities, they are also allowed and encouraged to use them during **You're the Teacher.** If they see a word they think is wrong, they may ask me how to spell it, and I will write it in their dictionary.

At the bottom of the page students are asked if they found a certain number of mistakes. They must answer yes or no. If students can't find all the mistakes and are intent on doing so, I will probably give them a hint by telling them the category the mistake is found in.

What about doing it together? With younger children or students with disabilities, use small groups. There is much mileage to be gained by letting students teach one another, and we should never forget that. I do make it clear, though, that students are to be teaching one another – not just giving the answers. So, how can we show students how to teach one another? Very simply – you send them to the board, and you sit with the students.

© 2009 Pieces of Learning
The Simple 6™ Revised Edition

Write these sentences on the board in advance.

my grandmother lives on elm street

when is are book order comming

my sister and i love cookies candie and cake

Students have already learned editing marks during English Wednesday mini-lessons, and they will now apply what they have learned to the sentences on the board.

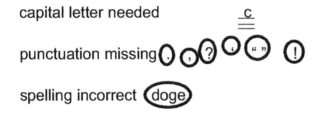

capital letter needed

punctuation missing

spelling incorrect doge

The student leader takes your place up front, calling on classmates to answer questions, come to the board to edit, and discuss reasons for why the corrections were necessary.

How should skills be chosen?

Teach, review, and focus on skills that are weak. These skills can easily be tracked if you add to a running list of grammatical errors every time you read student writing. This means spelling sentences, science tests, and mathematical word problems in addition to stories and essays. Re-teach the skills they need to practice.

Make it a point to check your academic standards for grammar several times throughout the year. This will guide instruction of new skills that should be introduced at this particular grade level.

The following pages provide an overview of standards for English mechanics at each grade level.

Language Arts Academic Standards for Grade 1

Students in Grade 1 will be able to:

Sentence Structure and Grammar

- write in complete sentences.
- use singular and plural nouns correctly.
- recognize and correctly write contractions.

Capitalization

- capitalize the first word in a sentence.
- capitalize names of people and the pronoun I.

Punctuation

- correctly use periods, exclamation points, and question marks at the end of sentences.

Spelling

- spell three and four-letter, phonetically-based words.
- spell correctly grade-level-appropriate sight vocabulary.

Tips: Students will use a ruler to focus on one sentence at a time. They will ask the following questions:

- Did the sentence begin with a capital letter?

- Are all the names in the sentence capitalized?

- Do I see any question words that will tell me this is not a statement?

- What kind of end mark do I need?

- Do any words look like they are spelled wrong?

Language Arts Academic Standards for Grade 2

Students in Grade 2 will be able to:

Sentence Structure and Grammar

- write in complete sentences.
- use correct word order in sentences.
- recognize and correctly write contractions.
- identify nouns and verbs in their sentences.

Punctuation

- correctly use periods, exclamation points, and question marks at the end of sentences.
- correctly use commas in the date, greeting, and closure of a friendly letter.
- correctly use commas in a series.

Capitalization

- capitalize the first word in a sentence.
- capitalize all proper nouns, focusing on months, days of the week, and titles.

Spelling

- spell phonetically-based words with long, short, and r-controlled vowel sounds.
- spell grade-level-appropriate sight vocabulary.
- spell words with beginning or ending consonant blends.

Tips: Students will use a ruler to focus on one sentence at a time. They will ask the following questions:

- Did the sentence begin with a capital letter?

- Are all the names in the sentence capitalized?

- Do I see any question words that will tell me this is not a statement?

- What kind of end mark do I need?

- Do I need any commas?

- Do any words look like they are spelled wrong?

Language Arts Academic Standards for Grade 3

Students in Grade 3 will be able to:

Sentence Structure and Grammar

- write complete declarative, imperative, interrogative, and exclamatory sentences.
- use subjects and verbs in agreement.
- use past, present, and future verb tenses correctly.
- write using adjectives and articles correctly.
- use pronouns and compound words correctly.
- use singular and plural possessive nouns correctly.

Punctuation

- correctly use periods, exclamation points, and question marks at the end of sentences.
- correctly use commas for dates, locations, and addresses.
- use quotation marks to show that someone is speaking.
- correctly use commas in a series, in compound sentences, and in direct quotations.

Capitalization

- capitalize the first word in a sentence.
- capitalize all proper nouns including geographical names, holidays, historical periods, and special events.

Spelling

- spell correctly one-syllable words with initial or final consonant blends.
- use common spelling patterns correctly, such as changing endings to add suffixes.
- spell common homonyms.
- spell correctly grade-level-appropriate sight vocabulary.

Tips: Students will use a ruler to focus on one sentence at a time. They will ask the following questions:

Did the sentence begin with a capital letter?	Is anyone speaking?
Are all the proper nouns in the sentence capitalized?	Are there any compound sentences?
What kind of ending punctuation do I need?	Does the verb agree with the subject?
Did I punctuate the parts of a friendly letter correctly?	Do any words look like they are spelled wrong?
Do any sentences need commas in a series?	
Do I see any question words that will tell me this is not a statement?	
Did I check to see if there were spelling changes due to word endings?	
Did I double check for homonyms being used correctly in the sentence?	

Language Arts Academic Standards for Grade 4

Students in Grade 4 will be able to:

Sentence Structure and Grammar

- write complete, simple and compound sentences.
- correctly use singular and plural possessive nouns.
- correctly use adjectives and adverbs.
- correctly use appositives and participial phrases.
- correctly use prepositional phrases.
- correctly use conjunctions.
- correctly use regular and irregular verbs, adverbs, and prepositions.

Punctuation

- correctly use periods, exclamation points, and question marks at the end of sentences.
- correctly use commas in the date, greeting, & closure of a friendly letter.
- use apostrophes in contractions and to show possession
- use quotation marks to show that someone is speaking or to identify titles of articles, short stories, poems, or chapters of books.
- underline or italicize titles of books, newspapers, magazines, works of art, and musical compositions.

Capitalization

- capitalize the first word in a sentence.
- capitalize all proper nouns, focusing on names of magazines, newspapers, works of art, musical compositions, organizations, and the first word in quotations, when appropriate.

Spelling

- spell base words, inflections, suffixes, prefixes, & individual syllables correctly.

Tips: Students will use a ruler to focus on one sentence at a time. Students will ask the following questions:

Did the sentence begin with a capital letter?	Are the proper nouns in the sentence capitalized?
What kind of ending punctuation do I need?	Did I punctuate the parts of a friendly letter correctly?
Do any sentences need commas in a series?	Did I use quotation marks in appropriate titles?
Is anyone speaking?	Did I underline appropriate titles?
Does the verb agree with the subject?	Do any words look like they are spelled wrong?

Did I check to see if there were spelling changes due to word endings?

Did I double check for homonyms being used correctly in the sentence?

Do I see any words that will tell me this is not a statement?

Are there any compound sentences, appositives, or participial phrases?

Language Arts Academic Standards for Grades 5

Grade 5 students will be able to:

Sentence Structure and Grammar

- write complex sentences that include prepositional phrases, appositives, main clauses and subordinate clauses.
- correctly use transitions and conjunctions.
- correctly use modifiers and pronouns.
- correctly use past, present, and future verb tenses.

Capitalization

- use correct capitalization.

Punctuation

- correctly use periods, exclamation points, and question marks at the end of sentences.
- correctly use commas.
- use a colon to separate hours and minutes and to introduce a list.
- correctly use quotations marks.
- correctly use semi-colons for transitions.

Spelling

- spell roots, prefixes, and suffixes correctly.
- spell syllable constructions correctly.
- spell common homonyms correctly.
- spell contractions correctly.

Tips: Students will use a ruler to focus on one sentence at a time. They will ask the following questions:

Did the sentence begin with a capital letter?

Are all the proper nouns in the sentence capitalized?

What kind of ending punctuation do I need?

Did I punctuate the parts of a friendly letter correctly?

Do any sentences need commas in a series?

Did I use quotation marks in appropriate titles? Is anyone speaking?

Did I underline appropriate titles?

Does the verb agree with the subject?

Do any words look like they are spelled wrong?

Did I check to see if there were spelling changes due to word endings?

Did I double check for homonyms being used correctly in the sentence?

Do I see any words that will tell me this is not a statement?

Are there any compound sentences, appositives, or participial phrases?

Language Arts Academic Standards for Grades 6

Grade 6 students will be able to:

Sentence Structure and Grammar

- write complete, simple, compound and complex sentences.
- use indefinite pronouns correctly.
- use verbs correctly in present perfect, past perfect, and future perfect tense.
- use correct verb agreement with compound subjects.

Capitalization

- use correct capitalization.

Punctuation

- correctly use periods, exclamation points, question marks, and commas.
- correctly use colons in the salutation of a business letter.
- correctly use semi-colons to connect main clauses.

Spelling

- spell correctly, including frequently misspelled words.

Tips: Students will ask themselves the following questions:

- Did I capitalize correctly?

- Is the sentence something other than a statement?

- Do complex sentences need commas for any reason?

- Did I punctuate correctly and include quotation marks if someone was speaking?

- Did I punctuate a friendly or business letter correctly?

- Does the verb agree with the subject?

- Have I corrected all misspelled words, including homonyms?

Language Arts Academic Standards for Grade 7

Grade 7 students will be able to:

Sentence Structure and Grammar

- properly place modifiers and use active voice.
- correctly use infinitives and participles.
- make clear references between pronouns and antecedents.
- demonstrate correct English usage.

Capitalization

- capitalize correctly.

Punctuation

- correctly use periods, exclamation points, question marks, and commas.
- correctly use hyphens, dashes, brackets, semicolons, and colons.

Spelling

- spell correctly, including frequently misspelled words.

Tips: Students will ask themselves the following questions:

Did I capitalize all proper nouns and sentence beginnings?

Did I use colons and semi-colons correctly?

Do complex sentences need commas for any reason?

Did I punctuate correctly (and include quotation marks) if someone was speaking?

Did I punctuate a friendly or business letter correctly?

Did I punctuate all the run-on sentences correctly?

Does the verb agree with the subject?

Do pronouns agree with their antecedents?

Were all modifiers punctuated correctly?

Have I reviewed the rules for commas, rather than placing them at random?

Have I corrected all misspelled words, including homonyms and spelling changes
      caused by new word endings?

Language Arts Academic Standards for Grade 8

Grade 8 students will be able to:

Sentence Structure and Grammar

- use correct and varied sentence patterns.
- write sentences with an effective personal style.
- use consistent elements of grammar when compiling a list.
- proofread and edit to ensure that correct grammar has been used.

Capitalization

- capitalize correctly.

Punctuation

- use correct punctuation.

Spelling

- spell correctly.

Tips: Students will ask themselves the following questions:

- Did I capitalize correctly?
- Is the sentence something other than a statement?
- Did I use colons and semi-colons correctly?
- Do complex sentences need commas for any reason?
- Did I punctuate correctly (and include quotation marks) if someone was speaking?
- Are items in a list parallel to one another?
- Did I punctuate a friendly or business letter correctly?
- Does the verb agree with the subject?
- Have I corrected all misspelled words, including homonyms?
- Did I watch out for commonly misused words?
- Have I proofread to make sure I found all errors?

Language Arts Academic Standards for Grades 9 and 10

Grade 9 and Grade 10 students will be able to:

Sentence Structure and Grammar

- write using standard English conventions.
- use correct and varied sentence patterns that illustrate an effective personal style.
- proofread and edit to ensure that correct grammar has been used.

Capitalization

- capitalize correctly.

Punctuation

- punctuate correctly.

Spelling

- spell correctly.

Tips: Students will ask themselves the following questions:

- Did I capitalize correctly?
- Is the sentence something other than a statement?
- Did I use colons and semi-colons correctly?
- Do complex sentences need commas for any reason?
- Are items in a list parallel to one another?
- Did I punctuate a friendly or business letter correctly?
- Does the verb agree with the subject?
- Have I corrected all misspelled words?
- Have I proofread to make sure I found all errors?

You're the Teacher:
Editing For Kids

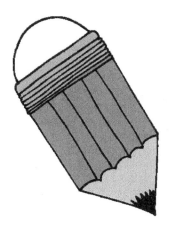

<u>You're the Teacher</u> worksheets, a set of 36 lessons for each grade level 1-8, are available in PDF form on separate CDs from Pieces of Learning. 1-800-729-5137.

Name _____ **Date** _____

You're the Teacher: Grade 1

1.   when will we go home

2.   i saw six grene frogs in that pond

3.   will you bring me fife cookies

4.   did susan finde her read hat

5.   how many kids kame to school today

6.   my dog's name is joe

7.   my sister is note very tall

8.   i wil eat an apple for lunch

Did you find 25 mistakes? _____

Hints: Look for words that need capital letters.
          Don't forget names.
          Add end marks.
          Fix misspelled words.

Name _____ **Date** _____

You're the Teacher: Grade 1

1. When will we go home(?)

2. I saw six ~~grene~~ *green* frogs in that pond(.)

3. Will you bring me ~~fife~~ *five* cookies(?)

4. Did Susan ~~finde~~ *find* her ~~read~~ *red* hat(?)

5. How many kids ~~kame~~ *came* to school today(?)

6. My dog's name is Joe(.)

7. My sister is ~~note~~ *not* very tall(.)

8. I ~~wil~~ *will* eat an apple for lunch(.)

Did you find 25 mistakes? Yes

Hints: Look for words that need capital letters.
          Don't forget names.
          Add end marks.
          Fix misspelled words.

Name _____ **Date** _____

You're the Teacher: Grade 2

1. there are six people in my family

2. my brother's name iz david

3. do you like brown elementary school

4. mr davis lives on maple avenue

5. isnt my littel kiten cute

6. sam has to cookies in his lunch

7. is your brithday in may

8. mike brung his football to school on friday

Did you find 33 mistakes? _____

Hints: Look for words that need capital letters
Add end marks to sentences
Correct any misspelled words.
(Watch out for number words!)

Name _____ **Date** _____

You're the Teacher: Grade 2

1. there are six people in my family.

2. my brother's name iz david.

3. do you like brown elementary school?

4. mr davis lives on maple avenue.

5. isnt my little kitten cute?

6. sam has two cookies in his lunch.

7. is your birthday in may?

8. mike brung his football to school on friday.

Did you find 33 mistakes? yes

Hints: Look for words that need capital letters
          Add end marks to sentences
          Correct any misspelled words.
          (Watch out for number words!)

Name _____ **Date** _____

You're the Teacher: Grade 3

1. who nose the answer two this problem

2. we went to wilsons market to by bread milk and soap

3. why don't it snow in florida

4. can you drawl a map of africa

5. jack seen about a hunderd gooses this morning

6. jennifers jacket is on the closet floor

7. megan brought a treet to school four the hole class

Did you find 33 mistakes? _____

Watch out for: proper nouns
question words
homonyms

Name _____ Date _____

You're the Teacher: Grade 3

1. who nose the answer two this problem?

2. we went to wilsons market to by bread, milk, and soap.

3. why don't it snow in florida?

4. can you draw a map of africa?

5. jack seen about a hunderd gooses this morning.

6. jennifers jacket is on the closet floor.

7. megan brought a treet to school four the hole class.

Did you find 33 mistakes? _yes_

Watch out for: proper nouns
                 question words
                 homonyms

Name _____ **Date** _____

You're the Teacher: Grade 4

1. can you see saturn through your telescrope

   asked susan

2. it takes the moon about a mouth to orbit this planet

3. mars jupiter and saturn are farther from the sun than

   earth

4. witch planet is the farthest from the son

5. all planets travel on a path called a orbit

6. what is your favorite planet asked matt

7. i see a shooting star yelled erik

Did you find 33 mistakes? _____

Watch out for: exclamatory sentences
                homonyms
                direct quotations

Chapter 6 Language in Use: The Four Point Rubric

Name _____ Date _____

You're the Teacher: Grade 4

1. "Can you see saturn through your telescope?

   asked susan.

2. It takes the moon about a month to orbit this planet.

3. Mars, jupiter, and saturn are farther from the sun than

   earth.

4. Which planet is the farthest from the sun?

5. All planets travel on a path called an orbit.

6. "What is your favorite planet?" asked matt.

7. "I see a shooting star!" yelled erik.

Did you find 33 mistakes? yes

Watch out for: exclamatory sentences
                  homonyms
                  direct quotations

© 2009 Pieces of Learning
The Simple 6™ Revised Edition

183

Name _____ **Date** _____

You're the Teacher: Grade 5

1. everyone was admiring lauries knew dog rocket

2. the famous statue of liberty stands proudly in the new york harbor

3. of coarse you can go to the movies replied mother

4. disneyland my favorite theme park is located in los angeles california

5. mr and mrs smith said there plain was leaving in a hour

6. has john finished writing his new mystery the secret of the missing key

7. i have only ate lunch in the cafeteria ten times this year

Did you find 50 mistakes? _____

Watch out for: proper nouns-places
titles
homonyms
direct quotations

Name _____ Date _____

You're the Teacher: Grade 5

1. everyone was admiring lauries (knew) dog rocket. [corrections: E, L, new, R, period]

2. the famous statue of liberty stands proudly in the new york harbor. [corrections: T, S, L, N, Y, H, period]

3. of (coarse) you (can) go to the movies replied mother. [corrections: O, course, may, comma marks, period]

4. disneyland my favorite theme park is located in los angeles california. [corrections: D, commas, L, A, C, period]

5. mr and mrs smith said (there)(plain) was leaving in (a) hour. [corrections: M, M, S, their, plane, an, period]

6. has john finished writing his new mystery the secret of the missing key? [corrections: H, J, "T, S, M, K, ?]

7. i have only (ate) lunch in the cafeteria ten times this year. [corrections: I, eaten, period]

Did you find 50 mistakes? _____

Watch out for: proper nouns-places
                   titles
                   homonyms
                   direct quotations

Name _____ **Date** _____

You're the Teacher: Grade 6

1. johns parents mr and mrs miller was allways taking pitchers of everyone

2. the conducter waves points and taps his batton

3. jacks favorite television show is the three stooges but they also enjoy watching jeopardy

4. me and tom apreciate the sounds made by a cello but we prefer the violin

5. if you dezired informasion about radiocarbon dating wear would you look

6. the old warn-out german shepherd loses its energy and died

7. if you live near a construction sight you may be able to observe some heavy machinery in action

Did you find 50 mistakes? _____

Watch out for: commas
                   homonyms
                   verb usage

Name _____ Date _____

You're the Teacher: Grade 6

1. ~~J~~ ~~(.)~~ **M** **M** **M** **were** **always** **pictures**
    johns parents mr and mrs miller (was) (allways) taking (pitchers)

    of everyone(.)

2. **T** **Conductor** **baton**
    the (conducter) waves points and taps his (batton) (.)

3. ~~J~~ ~~(.)~~ **T** **T** **S** ~~(")~~
    jacks favorite television show is the three stooges but they

    J **(.)**
    also enjoy watching jeopardy(.)

4. **Tom** **I** **appreciate**
    me and (tom) (apreciate) the sounds made by a cello but we

    prefer the violin(.)

5. **I** **desired** **information** **where**
    if you (dezired) (informasion) about radiocarbon dating (wear)

    would you look(?)

6. **T** **G** **S** **lost**
    the old warn-out german shepherd (loses) its energy and died(.)

7. **I** **site**
    if you live near a construction (sight) you may be able to

    observe some heavy machinery in action(.)

Did you find 50 mistakes? yes

Watch out for: commas
                  homonyms
                  verb usage

Name _____ **Date** _____

You're the Teacher: Grades 7 and 8

1.   since bill johns and david joseph are best freinds they have

     decided to room together in college

2.   did you no a bobsled team from jamaica competed in the

     olympics

3.   every one accept susan thomas was able to attend the

     concert

4.   do you think the aproaching rain clouds will effect our plans

     for the beach

5.   im surprised that youve all ready cut up the broccoli and

     cauliflouwer

6.   do you think its alright to put your elbows on the table while

     you eat

Did you find 33 mistakes? _____

Watch out for: commonly confused or misused words

Name _____ **Date** _____

You're the Teacher: Grades 7 and 8

1. since bill johns and david joseph are best freinds they have
   decided to room together in college.

2. did you no a bobsled team from jamaica competed in the
   olympics?

3. every one accept susan thomas was able to attend the
   concert.

4. do you think the aproaching rain clouds will effect our plans
   for the beach?

5. im surprised that you've all ready cut up the broccoli and
   cauliflouwer.

6. do you think its alright to put your elbows on the table while
   you eat?

Did you find 33 mistakes? yes

Watch out for: commonly confused or misused words

Name _____ **Date** _____

You're the Teacher: Grades 9 and 10

1. if youve ever visited its local campus you will see that ivy

    tech has a lot to offer its students

2. how much further is it before we get out of this dessert

3. i visited the american art museum and saw some extremely

    famous paintings

4. rebeccah and holly went to the boston book store on east

    85th street to get some stationary

5. it wasn't until I got to the end of the book that I realised it was

    part one of a two part series

6. to find out about conditions and membership details install

    the america online software

Did you find 33 mistakes? _____

Name _____ Date _____

You're the Teacher: Grades 9 and 10

1. if you've ever visited its local campus you will see that ivy
    tech has a lot to offer its students

2. how much further [farther] is it before we get out of this dessert [desert] ?

3. i visited the american art museum and saw some extremely

    famous paintings

4. rebeccah and holly went to the boston book store on east

    85th street to get some stationary [stationery]

5. it wasn't until I got to the end of the book that I realised [realized] it was

    part one of a two-part series

6. to find out about conditions and membership details install

    the america online software

Did you find 33 mistakes? yes

Chapter 7

Results:
The Proof is in the Scores

Committing One Grading Period

Nine Weeks at a Glance

Collecting and Analyzing the Data

Student Analysis Chart

Class Analysis Chart

Intervention Chart

Quarterly Data Analysis

Annual Student Data

Using the Data for Intervention, Remediation, and Encouragement

Celebrating Your Success and Spreading the Word

Chapter 7   Results: The Proof is in the Scores

Every class will improve.
That's the whole idea, isn't it?

In 1998, when this project began, 19% of the 6th graders in my school passed the standardized writing proficiency exam. It took time and commitment from many teachers, but we believed *The Simple 6*™ would work. By staying focused and encouraging our students every step of the way, we began to see steady improvement in student writing skills. After only one nine-week introduction to *The Simple 6*™, 51% **more** 6th graders passed than the year before. The scores were improving in other grades as well, but not all grade levels were evaluated using the standardized writing assessment.

By 2001, 80% of the 6th grade students were passing the standardized writing assessment. What's more impressive is the fact that these 6th graders were not just passing with a Score 4. 32% received a Score 5 or Score 6! More importantly, however, is the fact that only one student received less than a Score 3. (This special-needs student had an individualized education plan, and also showed growth from the baseline sample.) Are these statistics worth two hours of your time each week? Definitely!

Elementary students can recite the components of *The Simple 6*™, and they understand what each part means. They can score writing samples, they have an understanding of time management, and they approach standardized writing assessment with enthusiasm and confidence. The key to success is mere simplicity – putting the expectations into terms that students and teachers can understand.

Committing One Grading Period

Start the first day of school, the day after fall conferences, the first day back from winter break, or start tomorrow. This book is designed to get you started immediately. You just need to commit one, nine-week grading period to practice all the skills. The rest of the year can be spent writing, scoring, and continuing to improve.

On pages 194-196 is a thumbnail sketch of the activities your class will be doing during the nine weeks of instruction. Wednesday mini-lesson topics are suggestions only, as specific skill instruction will be determined by the needs of your individual class. The Weekly Writing Prompt may be derived from the lesson plans, but it will most likely be determined by the literature you are reading or the units of study you are engaged in through the content areas.

Nine Weeks at a Glance

Week 1: Stick to the Topic

Mini Lesson: Narrative or Descriptive Writing
Nouns: People, Places and Things

Thurs./Fri. Lesson: Using a noun subject, put ideas together that follow
a topic sentence. Introduce 3 Question Prompt Attack: body.

Writing Prompt:

Week 2: Logical Order

Mini Lesson: Expository Writing
First, Next, Then, and Finally
Beginning, Middle, End

Thurs./Fri. Lesson: Retell fairy tales, talk about "how to" paragraphs,
time lines, and ordering words like first, next, then,
and finally. Emphasize the importance of a strong
conclusion. Introduce Prompt Attack: introduction and
conclusion for a 3 question prompt.

Writing Prompt:

Week 3: Interesting Words

Mini Lesson: Descriptive Writing
Precise, Vivid Vocabulary
Adjectives, Synonyms

Thurs./Fri. Lesson: Replace generic vocabulary with at least 3 challenging
words.

Writing Prompt:

Week 4: Review, Share, and Revise

Mini Lesson: Review Narrative, Descriptive, and Expository
Writing
Revising and Editing
Three Challenging Words

Thurs./Fri. Lesson: Review the elements of sticking to the topic, having logical order
(with a strong conclusion), and including interesting words.
Think aloud as you model the writing process, starting with

brainstorming, organizing your thoughts, and writing a rough draft. Take a five-minute break, come back and continue with reading, revising, editing,and final drafting. All students should copy the final product. Review only what has been taught so far. Optional: Introduce What-Why Prompt Attack.

Shared Writing Sample(s):

Week 5: Different Sentence Patterns

Mini Lesson:	Descriptive Writing Compound Sentences, Sentences with Commas in a Series, Questions, Direct Quotations, Prepositional Phrases, Pronouns, Changing Word Order, Sentence Fluency
Thurs./Fri. Lesson:	List several sentences about the same topic. Show variety by changing word order, including questions, adding dialogue, and combining sentences.

Writing Prompt:

Week 6: Descriptive Sentences

Mini Lesson:	Descriptive Writing Precise Language, Using a Thesaurus, Appealing to the Reader's Senses, Painting a Vivid Picture, Supporting Details
Thurs./Fri. Lesson:	Talk about appealing to a person's senses. Add an experience if possible (like going outside during the first snow or heavy rain, eating an apple, carving a pumpkin, making cookie dough, running ten laps around the gym, etc.). The idea is to give the reader the same experience you are feeling and visualizing.

Writing Prompt:

Week 7: Audience

Mini Lesson:	Persuasive Writing Fact/Opinion Topic Sentence/Supporting Details/Conclusion Style/Voice
Thurs./Fri. Lesson:	Spend a day analyzing commercials to get students thinking about how methods of persuasion are used with an audience. Collect some "Letters to the Editor" from the local newspaper. Read them aloud to

students. Talk about difference in style, familiarity, enthusiasm and how it helps the interest level of the piece.

Writing Prompt:

Week 8: Peer Editing and Scoring

Mini Lesson: Rubric Scoring

Thurs./Fri. Lesson: Show the entire *Simple 6*™ rubric. Explain that for each part of the process you do well, you will get one point. Have samples at various scoring levels ready on overhead transparencies. Do the first one together. Give the same Score 3 sample to each small group to see how they revise differently but still show vast improvements.

Writing Sample(s):

Week 9: Creating a Score 6

Mini Lesson: Rubric Scoring
                      Review all Rubric Components:
                              Stick to the Topic
                              Logical Order
                              Interesting Words
                              Varied Sentence patterns
                              Descriptive Sentences
                              Audience

Thurs./Fri. Lesson: Share samples of exemplary writing. Give students an opportunity to work together or alone to create a passing paper.

Writing Prompt:

Collecting and Analyzing the Data

The nature of writing lends itself to having a lot of documentation. If you have organized and planned carefully, these documents should be stored in a place where you and your students can get to them easily and regularly. At the very least, you should now have six to eight writing samples from each student. If you chose to keep their prompt writing in a separate folder, you also have the dates, titles, and scores close by.

You now have access to valuable information. What are you going to do with it? Will you let students keep track of this collection of writing in their desks or lockers? Will you have a special place for their folders in the classroom? Will students be responsible for their own data collection? How will the information you collect be different from what they collect? Once you have all this stuff, what are you going to do with it?

Analyzing data is what gives teachers insight to diagnosing weaknesses and assisting students who need help. It is also important to remember that analysis of data shows us which students are capable of being exemplary writers. Keeping the data organized and readily available will allow the time to do the most important part – the analysis. As strange as it seems, most teachers don't make the time for this.

The basic data needed is on the progress sheet that is attached to the front of each student's writing folder. This sheet shows the dates, titles, and scores for each prompt. You may or may not want to document this information in a grade book, depending on the probability of being able to keep track of the writing folders. The diagnostic data, however, is found on the Student Analysis Chart. This chart can be filled out by the student each time a writing sample is returned. The information is derived from the mini-rubric that is attached to each piece of writing. It clearly shows which components the student has mastered and which still need instructional focus or continued practice. Consider the following examples:

Student Writing Progress for Bill Smith

Date	Topic	Order	Words	Patterns	Descrip-tions	Audience	Total
8-28	1	1					2
9-6	1	1				1	3
9-13	1	1	1			1	4
9-20	1	1		1			3

This student has an idea of how to organize a story or paragraph, but the message comes across in lower-level writing. Sentences lack interesting vocabulary, description, and any appeal to the senses. It is noteworthy that vocabulary increased during the week of instructional focus only. The same holds true for different sentence patterns. This student is eager to please but will probably need individual help and repetition of the strategies to increase his level of writing. Try not to give this student too many things to think about at the same time.

Student Writing Progress for Kim Jones

Date	Topic	Order	Words	Patterns	Descrip-tions	Audience	Total
8-28	1			1		1	3
9-6	1			1		1	3
9-13	1				1	1	3
9-20	1		1	1		1	4

This student is probably very personable. She likes to chatter and writes the way she speaks. She doesn't plan in advance. She just rambles, chatting amicably about various aspects of the topic. Her personality shines easily through her writing. She has the potential to be an outstanding writer because of her unique style, but she needs focus and organization.

Student Writing Progress for Ryan Davis

Date	Topic	Order	Words	Patterns	Descriptions	Audience	Total
8-28	1		1				2
9-6	1	1	1			1	4
9-13	1	1	1			1	4
9-20	1	1	1	1			4

This student is totally following your lead and shows cumulative strength in the areas as they are being introduced. Scores indicate that the student has the ability to be a proficient writer because of the constant use of higher-level vocabulary and the mastery of each skill as it is being presented. It also suggests that this student has had little instruction in writing and will steadily improve with practice and opportunity. I predict a Score 5 in the near future.

Student Writing Progress for David Johnson

Date	Topic	Order	Words	Patterns	Descriptions	Audience	Total
8-28	1	1					2
9-6	1	1				1	3
9-13	1	1			1		3
9-20	1	1			1		3

This student has imagination and a flair for writing, but has little sense of vocabulary (and spelling that makes you struggle to stay fluent as you read). This student has a knack for writing, but hasn't had the life experiences or reading expertise that is needed to put it all together. Encouraging this student to read about new places and experiences will help, as will just READING in general. Showing and discussing pictures will increase visual stimulation and give the student practice in verbalizing descriptions before writing them.

Sample Student Analysis Chart

Student Name : Karen Miller   **School year:** _____

Date	Topic	Order	Words	Patterns	Descrip-tions	Audience	Total
8-28	1		1				2
9-6	1	1	1			1	4
9-13	1	1	1		1		4
9-20	1	1	1	1	1		5

Date: _____   Observations/Conference with Student

Date: _____   Observations/Conference with Student

Date: _____   Observations/Conference with Student

Student Analysis Chart

Student Name:_____ **School year:** _____

Date	Topic	Order	Words	Patterns	Descrip-tions	Audience	Total

Date: _____ Observations/Conference with Student

Date: _____ Observations/Conference with Student

Date: _____ Observations/Conference with Student

Secondary Class Analysis Chart

TASK: __Favorite Person - Baseline__   DATE __8-15-07__

NAMES	TOPIC	ORDER	VOCAB	PATTERNS	DETAILS	AUDIENCE	TOTAL	
Barnett	1	1			1		3	
Barns	1	att. 1					2	frag.
Bogart	1	1	1		1		4	
Chamberlin	1	1	1	1		1	5	
Danaher	1	1			1		3	⌗
Gonzales	1	conc.			att. 1		2	sp.
Hannon	1	1	1	1			4	
Hartley	1	1	1	1	1		5	
Lazaridis	1	1		1			3	✓
Marczenko	1	1			1		3	
Naragon	1	1	1	1		1	5	
O'Hara	1	1		1	1		4	
Papaleo	1	1			1		3	⌗
Rodriguez	1	1			1		3	
Roggeman	Own	topic					0	
Salaiz	1	att. 1					2	sp.
Saros	1	1	1	1		1	5	
Scheu	1	1	1		1		4	
Soule	1	1		1	1		4	
Szuba	1	1	½		½		3	
Trkulja	Own	topic					0	
Varda	1	1	1		1		4	
Weaver	1	conc.		1			2	
Weber	1	1	1	1	1	1	6	
Zbrzezny	1	conc.	1	1			3	✓

Comments / Reflection:

Focus on the prompt.
Answer prompt questions.
Develop paragraphs.
Increase Vocab.

Strategies: Conclusion

✱ 2-page minimum

> homonyms
> Sent. fragments
> appositives

Class Analysis Chart

PROMPT: _____   DATE _____

Names	Topic	Order	Words	Patterns	Descrip-tions	Audience	Total

Comments / Reflection:

Intervention Chart

Identification and Strategies for Flexible Skill Groups

Skill: _____ Date Met: _____ Follow up: _____

Student Names:

1

2

3

4

5

6

Strategy discussed:

Skill: _____ Date Met: _____ Follow up: _____

Student Names:

1

2

3

4

5

6

Strategy discussed:

Teacher _____ Grade Level _____ # of Students _____

Quarterly School-wide Data Analysis for Writing

First Grade: Total Students _____
Average score per student (6 possible)   _____

Based on _____ prompts scores

% of students with a score of 4 or more   _____

Second Grade: Total Students _____
Average score per student (6 possible)   _____

Based on _____ prompts scores

% of students with a score of 4 or more   _____

Third Grade: Total Students _____
Average score per student (6 possible)   _____

Based on _____ prompts scores

% of students with a score of 4 or more   _____

Fourth Grade: Total Students _____
Average score per student (6 possible)   _____

Based on _____ prompts scores

% of students with a score of 4 or more   _____

Fifth Grade: Total Students _____
Average score per student (6 possible)   _____

Based on _____ prompts scores

% of students with a score of 4 or more   _____

Sixth Grade: Total Students _____
Average score per student (6 possible)   _____

Based on _____ prompts scores

% of students with a score of 4 or more   _____

Date _____   Total Number of Students _____

Annual Student Data: Writing Analysis Sample

Name : Susan Smith   **Grade Level**: Grade 6

Standardized Assessment Scores for Developmental Writing

Year	Assessment	Score/Possible
Last Year: 2007-2008	Developmental Writing	4 / 6
	Language in Use	4 / 4
Current Year:2008-2009	Developmental Writing	5 / 6
	Language in Use	4 / 4

Local Assessments for Quarterly Developmental Writing

	Topic	Order	Words	Patterns	Descrip-tions	Audience	Total
Baseline	1	1	1				3
Prompt 1	1	1	1	1			4
Prompt 2	1	1	1	1			4
Prompt 3	1	1	1	1	1		5
Final	1	1	1	1		1	5

Comments / Recommendations:

Skill group: descriptive sentences

Focus on appealing to the readers' senses, using prepositional phrases, and adjectives.

Skill group: audience

Focus on style and personality.

Emphasize questioning techniques and exclamations.

Mrs. Davidson
Teacher for Current Year

Annual Student Data: Writing Analysis

Name : _____   Grade Level: _____

Standardized Assessment Scores for Developmental Writing

Year	Assessment	Score/Possible
Last Year: _____	Developmental Writing	___ / ___
	Language in Use	___ / ___
Current Year: _____	Developmental Writing	___ / ___
	Language in Use	___ / ___

Local Assessments for Quarterly Developmental Writing

	Topic	Order	Words	Patterns	Descriptions	Audience	Total
Baseline							
Prompt 1							
Prompt 2							
Prompt 3							
Final							

Comments / Recommendations:

_____

Teacher for Current Year

Using the Data
for Intervention, Remediation, and Encouragement

With an upsurge in accountability, teachers find themselves collecting data at an alarming pace. Organization is critical, and routine procedures need to be commonplace. Analyzing writing progress is just one more thing in a long list of teacher responsibilities. Taking advantage of student assistance can help to manage the paperwork. Letting students lead a lesson or question their peers during a review solidifies their understanding of the concepts, gives them ownership in the process, and reinforces new skills.

Here are simple tips to help you stay focused and organized during the nine-week instructional experience.

1. Stay on a Thursday/Friday schedule. Keep the same time each day.

2. Establish a place for the writing folders.

3. Make sure students document writing tasks each week and keep samples in their folders.

4. Pay particular attention during informal observation. Is everyone participating?

5. Analyze the data each week.

6. Identify weaknesses by rubric component or individual student.

7. Conference with flexible skill groups and/or individuals weekly.

8. Praise students for their progress every step of the way.

9. Approach each lesson with enthusiasm and encouragement.

10. Step aside and let students take charge of the reviews and discussions.

11. Post a *Simple 6™* chart in your classroom, and refer to it every time students write.

12. Display writing samples and encourage students to share ideas with one another.

Celebrating Your Success and Spreading the Word

Once you and your students have experienced success, (and you will be successful) there are many things you can do to challenge others in your school or district.

School or District-wide Training in *The Simple 6*™ Method

Like students, teachers learn more effectively with guidance and interactive experiences. Training is available in *The Simple 6*™ methods of scoring writing assessments. For information contact KayDavidson6@aol.com

Peer Coaching between Classes

Peer coaching is successful with students of the same age. It is a unique opportunity for teachers of the same grade level to create flexible groups with more than one class. Peer coaching is also effective when older students teach the younger students. Groups as well as partners can change every week.

In-house Staff Development Sessions

Once one or several of your school's teachers become proficient in *The Simple 6*™ method, use staff development days to peer coach one another! Spend 10 minutes at each staff meeting trying one of the strategies or discussing those that have really encouraged students to write.

Monthly Grade Level Meeting Discussions

If your district has monthly grade level or department meetings, take that opportunity to review and discuss the components of *The Simple 6*™. Devise a grade-level plan that is vertically articulated throughout the school district. Share successes. Develop anchor papers for each grade level.

Analysis and Display of Data

Collecting data is meaningless if there is never an opportunity to study and analyze it. School administrators need to take a leadership role in providing guidance and opportunities for teachers to analyze, discuss, and display their data.

School Improvement Team Awareness

If your school has a School Improvement Team, those teachers on the Writing Committee would be responsible for collecting and comparing quarterly data, suggesting school-wide writing prompts, and offering praise and suggestions.

Quarterly Teacher-Principal Conferences

This is an opportunity for each teacher in the building to meet with the principal to discuss areas of concern or to share successes of the writing program. This meeting also gives teachers the extra push that is needed to compile the data each quarter and have it ready for presentation.

Classroom Writing Centers

Have many writing tools available. Notebooks, journals, chart paper, drawing paper, pictures, thesauruses, dictionaries, trade books, pencils, pens, markers, highlighters, and stickie notes should be in a Student Writing Center and readily available for use.

School-wide Writing Displays

Encourage all classes to display their writing: in their classrooms, outside their classrooms, in the cafeteria, in the principal's office, or any place else deemed appropriate. Schools may also choose to have a monthly or quarterly theme when all students write to similar prompts or about similar subjects.

Class/School Recognition Programs and Parties

Recognize students as soon as they have reached the "passing zone" or Score 4. When an entire class is scoring 4 and above, it's really time for a celebration. Check with your principal for grant money that may be available for rewards, or contact your local fast-food restaurant. Many will be glad to help you celebrate.

"Real" Publication

Every now and then writers surface in the classroom who have pieces that should be considered for "real" publication. There are many periodicals and journals that publish student work. You may also find that your public library would be happy to display exemplary writing during National Education Week or some other appropriate time. It never hurts to ask.

Students who become proficient at persuasive writing might want to write a letter to the editor of the local newspaper. They are always happy to include well-written student letters.

Parental Involvement

Using volunteers from the community increases 1:1 assistance, especially with young writers. Parents and grandparents are happy to listen to students read their stories. They can also be taught to ask strategic questions that encourage students to think and expand their writing experience.

District Recognition

Find a reason to celebrate writing across your school district. Monthly school board meetings are a wonderful opportunity to showcase the primary, intermediate, and secondary author of the month. A simple certificate is a great motivator and an indicator that writing is valued in the school district.

Young Authors' Conference

Many school districts or Reading Associations sponsor Young Authors' Conferences. Students of all ages attend the conference, bringing a piece of their best writing to share. They usually attend three sessions: one by a children's author, another by an illustrator, and a final session in which they are asked to share their work with their peers.

Writing Workshops

Writing workshops in the classroom are becoming increasingly popular with the emphasis on balanced literacy. Students are given regular opportunities to write. They are encouraged to make choices, take risks, and explore various aspects of writing. Work in progress is kept in an organizer so that students have easy access to pieces that they may want to take to the publishing stage.

Summer School Creative Writing Classes

Summer school is not just for remediation. Offering a creative writing class as a summer school option gives budding authors a chance to continue to write during the summer. It also allows them to meet new friends who are also interested in writing. A great culminating activity is to have every student submit something to a children's literary magazine.

Writing Buddies in Another School

What would be more fun than starting the school year with a pen pal in another school? As the year progresses, encourage students to share other pieces of their best writing, discuss novels or poetry, or offer writing topic ideas to one another. Meeting quarterly would give students a chance to meet, share their work, and have interactive writing projects or discussions.

Constantly Celebrate Success

It doesn't really take much to celebrate success. Simply telling your students they are becoming outstanding writers is an obvious place to start. An "Author of the Week" bulletin board, The 6 Club, an anthology of the best classroom stories, a Wonderful Writer certificate, and a piece of student writing in the weekly parent newsletter are all simple ways to constantly let students know you are proud of their progress.

The Simple 6:™ A Writing Rubric for Kids is designed for success in every classroom. It gives students a clear understanding of what is expected in an exemplary piece of writing. Not only does its concrete, no-nonsense approach easily guide teachers through classroom writing instruction, but it clearly offers solutions to problems with organization, time management, and data collection.

Nine years of action-research data provide results that illustrate the program's impact on classroom instruction. By focusing on analysis and simplicity, *The Simple 6™* brings excitement, encouragement, and understanding to teachers and students as they strive for mastery of written expression.

Any teacher's class can master ***The Simple 6***™. If you make the commitment and encourage your students every step of the way, they will soon be passing writing assessments with ease!

Bibliography

Andrade, Heidi Goodrich. "Using Rubrics to Promote Thinking and Learning." *Educational Leadership*. Alexandria, Virginia: ASCD, February, 2000.

"Annual School Performance Report." *South Bend Tribune*. South Bend, Indiana. September 13, 1999.

Assessment Scale for Grades 2-5. http://www.powayusd.sdcoe.K12.ca.us/jkajita

Coil, Carolyn. *Teaching Tools for the 21st Century*. Marion, Illinois: Pieces of Learning, 2000 rev.

Coil, Carolyn and Merritt, Dodie. *Solving the Assessment Puzzle Piece by Piece*. Marion, Illinois: Pieces of Learning, 2001.

Danielson, Charlotte. *A Collection of Performance Tasks and Rubrics: Upper Elementary School Mathematics*. Larchmont, New York: Eye on Education, Inc., 1997.

Davidson, Kay. *Becoming a Better Writer Using The Simple 6™ 3rd-6th*. Marion IL. Pieces of Learning. 2007. Complementary CD also available
    The Simple 6™ for Beginning Writers. Marion IL. Pieces of Learning. 2007. Complementary CD also available.
    The Simple 6™ for Secondary Writers. Marion IL. Pieces of Learning. 2008.CD also available.
    You're the Teacher: Editing for Kids. Grade 1, Grade 2, Grade 3, Grade 4, Grade 5, Grade 6, Grade 7, Grade 8 each on CD Rom. Marion IL: Pieces of Learning, 2004.

Digest of Education Statistics. Chapter 2: *Elementary and Secondary Education, 2000*. http://www.nces.ed.gov/pubs2001/digest/ch.2

Hurst, David S., Presenter. "Enhancing the Quality of Students' Work Using Rubrics." North Mankato, Minnesota: Ten Sigma, Inc.,1998.

Kemper, Dave, Nathan, Ruth, Sebranek, Patrick. *Writers Express: A Handbook for Young Writers, Thinkers, and Learners*, United States: D. C. Heath and Company, 1995.

Kemper, Dave, Meyer, Verne, and Sebranek, Patrick. *Write Source 2000: A Guide to Writing, Thinking, and Learning*, United States: D. C. Heath, and Company, 1995.

Kemper, Dave, Nathan, Ruth, Sebranek, Patrick. *Write on Track: A Handbook for Young Writers, Thinkers, and Learners*, United States: D. C. Heath and Company, 1996.

Learning Network. *Assessment: The Advantages of Rubrics*. http://www.teachervision.com

Learning Network. *Assessment: Analytic vs. Holistic Rubrics.* http://www.teachervision.com

Leber, Sally Speer. *Writing to Describe*, Columbus: Zaner-Bloser, Inc., 1997.

Leber, Sally Speer. *Writing to Inform*, Columbus: Zaner-Bloser, Inc., 1997.

Leber, Sally Speer, *Writing a Narrative*, Columbus: Zaner-Bloser, Inc. 1997.

Leber, Sally Speer. *Writing to Persuade*, Columbus: Zaner-Bloser, Inc., 1997.

McCaig, Roger A. *Learning to Write: A Model for Curriculum and Assessment*, Fourth Edition, Grosse Pointe, Michigan: The Grosse Point Public School System, 2000.

McCarthy, Tara, *Descriptive Writing*, New York: Scholastic Professional Books, 1998.

McCarthy, Tara, *Expository Writing*, New York: Scholastic Professional Books, 1998.

McCarthy, Tara, *Narrative Writing*, New York: Scholastic Professional Books, 1998.

McCarthy, Tara, *Persuasive Writing*, New York: Scholastic Professional Books, 1998.

National Center for Education Statistics. *The Nation's Report Card: Writing*. National Assessment of Educational Progress (NAEP). 1998 Writing Assessment. http://www.nces.ed/gov/naep3/writing/stateachlvls.asp

Phillips, Gary W. "Statement on Long-Term Trend Writing NAEP. National Center for Education Statistics, April 11, 2000. http://www.nces.ed.gov/commissioner/remarks2000

Popham, W. James. "What's Wrong and What's Right with Rubrics?" *Educational Leadership*, October 13, 2001.

Rose, Lowell. "Not Making the Grade." *South Bend Tribune*, South Bend, Indiana. September 12, 2001.

Samara, John and Curry, James. *The Curriculum Project*. Austin, Texas: Middle School Curriculum Institute,1992.

"School Corporation Annual Performance Report." *South Bend Tribune*. South Bend, Indiana. September 14, 2001.

State of California Department of Education, *STAR Test Results*, 2003. http://www.ca.gov./statetests/star/resources.html.

State of Colorado Department of Education, *Analytic Rubric for the Extended Constructed Response*, 2001. http://www.cde.state.co.us/cdeassess/as.write.ECRubric.htm

State of Colorado Department of Education, *Holistic Writing Rubric for the Short Constructed-Response Task*, 2001.

http://www.cde.state.co.us/cdeassess/as.write.ECRubric.htm

State of Florida Department of Education, *Florida Writing Assessment Program: Florida Writes!, 2003.* http://www.firn.edu/doe/sas/fw/fwapachv.htm

State of Illinois Department of Education, Illinois Learning Standards for English Language Arts, 2003. http://www.isbe.state.il.us/assessment/default/htm.

State of Indiana Department of Education, Indiana Academic Standards for Language Arts, 2000. http://www.doe.state.in.us/

State of Indiana Department of Education, Teacher's Scoring Guide ISTEP+: Grade 3, Grade 6, Grade 10. CTB/McGraw-Hill, Monterey, California. 1997, 1999, 2000.

State of Michigan Department of Education. *Communication Arts: Writing, Model of the Assessment.* Michigan Educational Assessment Program, 1995.

State of New York Department of Education. *Elementary and Intermediate State Assessments for the 2001-2002 School Year.* Office of State Assessment, 2001. http://www.emsc.nysed.gov/ciai/testing/elsche.htm

State of Ohio Department of Education, Ohio Writing Project, 2002. http://www.units.muohio.edu/owp/sa.html.

State of Pennsylvania Department of Education, Pennsylvania Writing Assessment, 2002. http://www.ccsso.org./assessment/html.

State of Tennessee Department of Education. Tennessee Anytime. *Tennessee Writing Assessment Scoring Rubric.* http://www.state.tn.us/education/tswriting

State of Wisconsin Department of Education, *Wisconsin Student Assessment System: Writing Exemplar Booklet: Knowledge and Concepts Examinations for Grades 4, 8, and 10.* Wisconsin Department of Public Instruction, adapted from CTB-McGraw-Hill School Publishing Company, 1993.

U.S. Department of Education. The Common Core of Data (CCD). National Center for Education Statistics. http://www.nces.ed.gov/ccd

U.S. Department of Education. *National Institute on Student Achievement, Curriculum and Assessment.* Washington, D.C.: Office of Educational Research and Improvement, 2001.

U.S. Department of Education. What's Wrong with Writing and What Can We Do Right Now? April, 1993. Washington, D.C.: Office of Educational Research and Improvement. http://www.ed.gov/pubs